Shin'ichi Suzuki

Nurtured by Love

REVISED EDITION

Translated from the Original Japanese Text

Translated by Kyoko Selden with Lili Selden

Produced by
Alfred Music Publishing Co., Inc.
P.O. Box 10003
Van Nuys, CA 91410-0003
alfred.com

Printed in USA.

AMPV 1.0 with index

ISBN-10: 0-7390-9044-5
ISBN-13: 978-0-7390-9044-2

Preface

In society today, a tremendous number of people seem resigned either to the belief that they can achieve nothing because they are incapable by birth, or to accepting the way they are as a matter of fate. As a result, they spend their days unable to experience a vivid happiness, a soul-satisfying joy. This, one must say, is the greatest misfortune to befall a human being.

Human ability is not innate. All children, at birth, are endowed by Nature with a life force that stirs in them a will to live. As I have continuously stated throughout my thirty-some years of experience, these children then acquire their individual abilities, in accordance with the workings of that life force, and in the course of adapting to the environment in which they have been placed.

Many people in the real world are mis-educated, not having been provided with an environment conducive to developing their abilities. Moreover, their shortcomings are ascribed by those around them to their inferior birth, and they themselves share that judgment. This is all wrong.

Although the Talent Education movement in which I have been engaged for the past twenty years is properly understood in foreign countries, it is still viewed in Japan as a kind of prodigy education. If you read this book, however, you will instantly understand that that is simply not the case. I believe you will also be persuaded that people who are unappealing have become so because they were raised by unappealing people, and others who are incapable have become so because they were raised by incapable people.

I cannot deny the thing called fate. This is because the very fact that any of us was born into this world, like the fact that we will eventually die, is something about which we can do nothing. However, for better or for worse, once we have become adults, we must live by our own strength until the day we die. And thus, the unavoidable question arises of how we ought to live. Ability that has not been fostered is something we have to create on our own. Rather than succumbing to adverse luck, we should turn our lives to the better. We must not give up; nor is there any need to give up. This is something that is within the reach of every person, each in his or her own way. Indeed, it is to make this very claim that I have written this book. And so . . .

Chapter 1 explains how human ability develops, Chapter 2 relates how one ordinary child developed into a generous-minded and skilled performer, and Chapter 3 discusses with concrete examples what a person can do to turn incapability to capability, the ordinary to the extraordinary. If someone were to challenge me, asking, "Well, what about you, what have you done for yourself?" Chapters 4 and 5 would answer their question. Chapter 6, then, emphasizes "action," without which, all reasoning aside, one can get nowhere. In Chapters 7 and 8, I feel a certain pleasure at being able to share anecdotes regarding our Talent Education Method for violin instruction, and the achievements it has produced.

Full of life, a tree puts forth buds, and flowers bloom beautifully up and down its branches. And human life unfolds in precisely the same way as these activities occur in Nature; I always reflect on this marvel. What, then, is the ultimate form to be attained by this human life force? It is to love everything and never stop seeking truth, goodness, and beauty. This is true for myself, and also for you.

I would be delighted if this book could be of any help in nourishing that which our souls seek. I extend my deep gratitude to Yamamoto Yasuo and Fujii Kazuko, at Kōdansha Publishing, for supporting my wishes regarding this volume.

June, 1966

As I prepare for a lecture tour of the United States,

Suzuki Shin'ichi

Table of Contents

The names of Japanese individuals are consistently given in the Japanese style, with family names first, except in the case of the author on the title page. For example, in the name Toyoda Kōji, Toyoda is the family name and Kōji the personal name. Macrons are used for Japanese long vowels throughout except in well-known place names like Tokyo and Osaka.

Prologue:
A Day of Marveling

Children Throughout Japan Speak Japanese!

"Ohh! Children everywhere in Japan are speaking Japanese!"

I leaped up in astonishment. Each and every child speaks Japanese freely, and they do so without any difficulty whatsoever. Isn't this a marvelous ability? Why is this? How has this come to pass? I could barely suppress my impulse to run into the streets, shouting.

For about a week following this revelation, I spoke to everyone I met.

"All children throughout Japan speak Japanese magnificently. Children from Osaka speak that difficult Osaka dialect, and children from the Northeast speak that Northeastern dialect we could never even hope to reproduce. Isn't this incredible?"

But nobody was impressed. It's a matter of course, everyone said. Instead of being surprised by the fact that every child demonstrates such ability, people were half surprised and half appalled by the fuss I was making about something that is common sense.

However, this discovery of mine held enormous significance for me. It happened one day over 30 years ago, when I was 33 or 34. And this discovery not only solved a problem I was confronting at the time but came to form the basis that determined my life thereafter.

I believe it was around 1931. I was teaching only youths at the Teikoku and Kunitachi Music Academies, but a four-year-old boy appeared at my door, accompanied by his father. It was Etō Toshiya, now a fine violinist.[1]

---

[1] Teikoku Music Academy (Teikoku Ongaku Gakkō) was established in 1931 with Suzuki Shin'ichi as co-founder. The word *teikoku* means "imperial" but the school was not state run. The school also predates the Reichsmusikkammer (Teikoku Ongaku Gakuin in Japanese), which was founded by Joseph Goebbels in Germany in 1933. Teikoku Music Academy was closed in 1944 because of war damage. Kunitachi Music Academy, now Kunitachi College of Music, was founded in 1926 as the Tokyo Higher Academy of Music.

Whence This Marvelous Phenomenon?

Having brought along the four-year-old Toshiya, his father said, "I'd like to entrust my child to you." He was asking me to teach his son the violin. I was at a complete loss as to how I ought to nurture such a young child, or what I might teach him. I had never had such an experience.

What kind of approach would serve me best in teaching a four-year-old? I pondered this question day and night.

That became the starting point leading to my discovery. At the time, my brothers and I had formed a quartet, and one day while we were rehearsing at my younger brother's place, it flashed into my head: every child throughout Japan speaks Japanese.

For me, that realization was the proverbial light on a moonless night.

Children freely speak Japanese, I realized, because they are, in effect, given the opportunity to do so. There is the fact of training and education behind their capacity to speak. Therein lay a proper educational method. Every child, without question, is developing appropriately. This was precisely that perfect educational method I was seeking. An educational method that ensured the development of Japanese children already existed everywhere in Japan.

My awakening to this fact left me astonished.

Children who are called dull because they are poor at math, too, speak Japanese with absolute freedom. This is strange, is it not? The reason for their ineptitude at math, then, is not that they are dull. What is at fault is the method by which they are being taught. It is not that these children have no talent, but rather that their talent has not been cultivated.

Yet another surprise for me was that nobody else was aware of this fact despite its being clearly visible before human eyes since ancient times. Nevertheless, what made me leap up in amazement was another fact even prior to that one. When I tried organizing my thoughts, I came up with the following.

Herein Lie the Keys to Developing Ability

(1) As far as mother-tongue education goes, children who earn low marks at school and are called dull by birth have acquired superior ability to speak Japanese.

(2) In other words, an educational method for successful development has been applied to every child. Contained among the pedagogical conditions of first-language acquisition that are in effect from the day a child is born, I found, was a method to overshadow every other painstakingly thought-out method.

(3) All children, without exception, flourish in response to skillful teaching. They are born equipped with that potential.

Here, I thought, was the key to human development, or more precisely, ability development. I had unexpectedly run into a wall upon being asked to teach the four-year-old Etō Toshiya, and having thought every which way through the challenge, I now awoke with tremendous excitement to this "mother-tongue educational method."

Fueled by my certain belief that every child thrives, I have worked continuously for 30-odd years within an educational movement that creates no dropouts, and that I have named "Talent Education." That day of wonderment became the start of my inquiry into humanity. As to where that path has led me, I would like to discuss it as enjoyably and concretely as possible, while reflecting on the past and hoping for the future.

A group lesson at the Matsumoto Academy of Music.

1

Ability Is Meant to Be Fostered

Dr. Suzuki with children.

– 1 –
Ability Begets Ability

Time and Stimulation as Factors Ensuring the Burgeoning of Ability

The Shinagawa Chapter of the Talent Education Institute in Tokyo boasts the presence of Pīko, a pet for the young children who come there for violin lessons. Miyazawa Susumu, the instructor there, keeps this parakeet with his wife.

The Miyazawas untiringly teach Japanese to this bird.

"I am Miyazawa Pīko, I am Miyazawa . . . "

The bird repeats this in a high-pitched voice, to which the children respond, "Oh, Pīko, you're so sweet! You're such a sweetheart!" Here is what Mr. Miyazawa says about Pīko's abilities:

As you might expect, you have to start soon after birth. At first it takes a great deal of patience. For the parakeet's verbal abilities to sprout, you must repeat the same words again and again. Things start so slowly that you may easily find yourself discouraged and wanting to abandon your efforts.

The first thing was naming her Pīko and teaching her the name about 50 times daily. Over a period of two months, we must have repeated it to her 3,000 times. Only then did she finally start to say "Pīko." My guess is that before she was able to say it, she needed time for the ability to sprout within her and then to manifest itself externally. That was a preparatory period requiring time and stimulation from the environment. When we plant seeds, even though we can't see what's happening, they transform themselves underground, little by little every day in response to the combined stimuli of water and warmth, plus light and dark, until one day they finally sprout. It must be the same with a parakeet too.

The Wondrous Blooming of Development

But once it sprouts, Mr. Miyazawa continues, the bird's development picks up speed gradually.

When Pīko was able to say "Pīko" after those 3,000 repetitions on our part, we added our family name, "Miyazawa." This time, however, Pīko was able, within 200 repetitions, or one-fifteenth of the time it took for her to reproduce the sound "Pīko," to say "Miyazawa Pīko."

It is certainly the same with human beings: no matter what the activity, we go slowly at first. The process of acquiring an ability is a time-consuming one. But it is an undeniable fact that abilities, once acquired, develop into yet higher abilities. Whenever we give up, thinking we are going nowhere, the abilities that have started developing nicely wilt away before they have a chance to manifest themselves externally. We must therefore patiently continue to repeat our training, so as to allow abilities to blossom. On the basis of having trained Pīko, we have fully come to realize the truth of this insight.

Ability begets ability—this was demonstrated in Pīko later on as well. She began to utter a number of other words. She also reproduces in a lovely voice the first measure, "takataka tatta," of the "Twinkle Variations" the children play on the violin. Abilities, once generated, foster more ability, while also gaining speed; the increased abilities in turn operate to add further speed, developing into new, higher levels of ability. It was interesting when I had a cold and coughed every day. Sporadically each day Pīko said, "I am Miyazawa Pīko, cough cough."

Mr. Miyazawa's story offers proof, through a parakeet, to support my faith in ability development. I hold him in great regard for the way he nurtures children while impressing upon himself that even a bird can likewise be trained in this manner.

A Baby's Eyes

This next episode took place 14 years ago, in the spring of 1952. At an acquaintance's home in Ueda, Shinshū[1], I was having a pleasant conversation with local members of the Talent Education Institute. At one point, the Shimada and Kiuchi children arrived with their small violins.

"Okay, let's have fun playing together," we decided. As usual, the children played through various pieces, in unison, with great glee.

Just before me was a baby nestled in Mrs. Kiuchi's arms. On questioning, I learned that the infant was named Hiromi, and that she was five months old.

At the time, Hiromi's older sister Atsumi, age six, was daily practicing Vivaldi's Concerto in A Minor, as well as listening to a recording of the concerto. This meant that Hiromi was growing up hearing that piece every day. Curious as to how that might impact a five-month-old baby, I rose and said, "This time let me play a little something." I pulled out my violin, and when everyone had quieted down I began by playing a Bach minuet. I kept my eyes glued to Hiromi the entire time I played.

The five-month-old, who already knew the sound of the violin, responded with alertly shining eyes to this piece she was hearing for the first time ever. Several phrases into the piece, however, I segued without a break into the Vivaldi A minor, which her older sister Atsumi was practicing every day. In that moment, before I had even finished playing the first measure of the Vivaldi, an amazing thing occurred.

---

[1] Shinshū (the Sinized form of "Shinano province") is the traditional name, still in common use, for today's Nagano prefecture, or jurisdiction.

Spiritual Joy Filling Her Entire Body

Hiromi's expression suddenly changed; she flashed a momentary smile, and then, truly joyfully, she turned around to look at her mother holding her. She seemed to say, "Oh, it's that piece I know!" Her mother nodded back at her. Hiromi immediately turned around to face me again. And this time, perhaps wanting to beat time to the piece, she jiggled her body up and down. Five months after birth, she knew the Vivaldi concerto and its melody inside out. In effect, young children adapt to their environment, unconsciously absorbing what they see and hear as they grow, and in this manner forming their personalities—I sensed that I was observing a strikingly vivid example of this process. It is an almost terrifying fact, one that is emphatically not limited to spoken language or music.

Four years passed since then.

It was at a concert in Matsumoto. On stage were 150 young children, beautifully playing in unison on their pint-sized violins. The piece was Vivaldi's *Concerto in A Minor*.

"Who is that four- or five-year-old," I was irresistibly compelled to ask the instructor leading the class, "playing at the center of the front row?"

The child was playing with so much enthusiasm that I had opened my mouth before I even knew it. With excellent posture, and with overflowing joy expressed in every fiber of her being, she was playing the concerto with great verve.

"That's Kiuchi Hiromi from Ueda city."

"Oh, so that's her . . . that child . . . No wonder, I see, no wonder . . . "

That baby Hiromi, whom I had seen at five months of age, had indeed flourished beautifully and with spontaneity in a joyous milieu.

This Is the True Happiness of a Human Child

Yet another 10 years passed. Hiromi, now a junior high school student, sent me a musical score with a letter.

> Dear Mr. Suzuki,
>
> I composed a piece to go with a poem I wrote, and placed first in an All Japan Elementary and Junior High School Composition Competition called "Our Songs." Please take a look.

Perusing the music, I found a richly sensitive poem and score. When I think back over a dozen years to the baby in her mother's lap, happily bouncing in time to the Vivaldi concerto I was playing, I realize afresh that beautiful and exceptional humanity, and ability as well, can develop to such heights depending upon how the parents go about fostering their child.

This is not a question of whether a child will become a musician or an artist. I am simply pondering the happiness of Atsumi and Hiromi, born the same as any other human being but fostered in such an exemplary manner.

In each individual human being is inscribed the person's history, including her abilities, sensory perceptions, and heart. Carefully look at each person's face and eyes. You will find reflected in them the history of that particular individual's daily life, leading up to that very day, as well as her character in its entirety. Additionally, that historical imprint changes hour by hour along with the person's life course.

Such are the delicate workings of our life forces.[2] As I state below, we all inevitably run up against the question of how to live. For now, however, let me continue awhile longer on the matters of how children develop, and how to assist that development.

---

[2] The expression for "life forces" here is *seimei,* made up of the Chinese characters "sei" (生, meaning "to live" or "to be alive") and "mei" (命, meaning "life" or "destiny"). The compound word can denote "a life time," "life," "life force," "essence," and so forth. It is often simply translated as "life" in this book, but at times as "life force" as here. The author also frequently uses the expression *seimeiryoku* (生命力), "life force" or "vitality."

– 2 –
Ability Is Not Innate

The Fate of a Warbler Is Determined in Its First Month

The Japanese bushwarbler with its beautiful voice and its masterful warbling—I used to consider those celebrated features hereditary. I believed, in other words, that the offspring of a master bushwarbler inherited the predisposition of its parents. However, that turns out not to be the case.

In spring, the warbler trainer enters the mountains to find a wild bushwarbler's nest. Catching and bringing home a young bird still being cared for by its parents, the trainer coaxes the fledgling to acclimate to being fed by humans. Timing the moment when it has gotten used to its new diet and generally has calmed down, he borrows a master bushwarbler from elsewhere and exposes the young bird on a daily basis to the master's beautiful warbling. This period lasts approximately one month.

The above process of cultivating wild young birds, with the aim of turning them into master warblers, is a method practiced from long ago in Japan. To raise the young *in a supreme environment*—in other words, this is Talent Education for warblers. The young bird to be trained in this manner is called *tsukego*, or "attached child," perhaps meaning a fledgling attached to a teacher bird.

The *tsukego* receives careful education in a variety of forms after that initial period. However, what is vital above and beyond all else is to attach it to a good teacher in that first month. For indeed, the very future of the young bird is determined by the superiority or inferiority of its teacher's vocal quality and melodic phrasing. In other words, there is no innate superiority or inferiority. What is there is the young bushwarbler's life force. The operation of that life force has a marvelous power through which the bird strives to adapt to its environment, enabling it to undergo physiological changes that allow it to foster the ability to utter beautiful sounds, acquire a masterful delivery, and, by the time it is full-fledged, warble with the same beautiful voice and turns of phrase as those of its teacher.

Based on empirical evidence, however, it has been said from long ago that the attempt always fails when the apprentice bird has already been exposed to the singing of wild bushwarblers. This illustrates the law of ability formation among living creatures in the natural world. Is it possible that this example relating to the cultivation of young birds proffers a valuable hint for ability development in human beings as well? At least for me, the belief that this might indeed be the case has provided tremendous strength and confidence in my approach to nurturing children.

Making Children Tone Deaf the World Over

Based on the rule of ability formation in living beings that we have observed in the example of bushwarblers, let's look at one aspect of ability formation in human children. I often hear people say, "I'm a tone-deaf parent, so . . . " The claim is that therefore the child is tone deaf and nothing can be done because this is a matter of heredity. However, I would suggest that just as there is no such thing as an innately tone deaf warbler, there does not exist an innately tone deaf human child.

Far from being tone deaf, all infants have marvelous hearing. That is why they unerringly absorb the off-key pitches of the lullabies sung to them by their tone deaf parents. The process is exactly identical to that of Osaka children, who without exception master the delicate melody of Osaka dialect.

It is thus clear that recording a horribly out-of-tune song and playing it daily for a group of babies will render every single one of them tone deaf. In other words, if we wished to do so, we could turn all children throughout the world tone deaf. Given that such a plan could successfully be carried out, there assuredly cannot be such a thing as inborn musical talent.

These insights carry an enormous significance, speaking as they do to the following points:

(1) How a human being develops ability in the process of growing up;

(2) Not limited to music, never is a single talent innate.

Kamala, Amala, and Their Fostering by Wolves

Human ability is not innate. The true configuration of human formation—that is to say, the fact that our life forces endeavor to cause us to adapt to our environment, thereby enabling us to acquire ability—is unequivocally known from the following valuable resource, among others. I summarize here from "Girls Fostered by Wolves," an account by Dr. Kida Fumio published in *Child Psychology* (Volume 3, Issue 9).

A record of great consequence was publicized in 1941 by two professors, one from the University of Denver and the other from Yale University. The record consisted of a nine-year-long detailed observation log and its accompanying photos by a certain Father Singh, who took over the care of two children discovered in India to have been fostered by wolves.

Both were girls, the one approximately two years old, the other seven. Father Singh named the younger one Amala, and the older one Kamala. They had been found in the jungles inhabited by the Kola tribe to the southwest of Calcutta. When first sighted, the two children had long, thick hair on their heads, chests, and shoulders. Once that hair was trimmed, the girls looked very much more human.

Among certain aboriginal peoples in India, it is said, baby girls are often abandoned. These two abandoned children were apparently picked up separately by one and the same female wolf, which had such a proclivity, and they were fostered in her den for seven and two years, respectively, along with other wolves and nursing siblings.

Four-Legged Mobility and Nightly Howling at a Fixed Hour

In the wolf's den, the children moved about on all fours, and they developed night vision as well as a keen sense of smell. When running on all fours, they were as fast as dogs, and no human could keep up with them.

They had broad, strong shoulders, and their legs bent at the crotch, unable to straighten out. To grab hold of things, they used their mouths rather than their hands, and they took food and water in the manner of dogs. Kamala, in whom a wolf-like mode of being was particularly ingrained, not only loved raw meat but showed signs of being strongly drawn to rotting meat as well.

Accustomed to variations in temperature, the girls never perspired when it was hot, but instead hung out their tongues and panted like dogs. Their skin was smooth and did not pick up dirt, and they had calluses on their palms from walking on them. Their hair was long and entangled, their heads abnormally large. Additionally, they responded with alert tension to noises, and when angered flared their nostrils and growled like dogs. If anyone interrupted while they were eating, they bared their teeth and barked.

The girls slept or lay around during the day, only becoming active when the sun went down. Wolves in that region had the habit of howling to one another three times after dark, and, moreover, at approximately the same times nightly: at ten, at one, and at three. Kamala and Amala, too, howled in unison with this recurring howling. Indeed, Kamala continued her night-time howling for nine years, despite every effort to stop her, until her death at age 16. Her voice had a peculiar quality that was hard to characterize either as human or beastly.

Can We Still Insist That Ability Is "Innate"?

Here were two human children who lived among, and were raised by, wolves, and who in the process acquired the lifestyle habits of those wolves. I feel awed by the natural law by which we humans live while adapting to our environments—by the almost solemn power of our life forces, which activate themselves in order for us to survive.

This fact vividly conveys how the world's children try to live by means of their life forces, and how each and every human being develops. It poignantly counsels us to discard every notion of what we have believed until now to be innate, including our hearts, sensibilities, wisdom, and conduct.

The state into which Kamala and Amala were reared is utterly tragic by human standards. When the two were brought back from their lives among wolves to human society, people judged them to be feeble-minded. I must point out, however, that that represents a negative assessment formed by comparing the outcome of their upbringing with those of children who have only known human society. Kamala and Amala, who adapted to the life habits of wolves, despite being human children, were each endowed with an outstanding life force and a natural superiority; had they been raised in a properly civilized environment, I am certain they would have attained extremely high levels of development.

Naturally this is no more than a hypothesis. However, surely even the most obstinate exponent of innate-ability theory would hesitate to describe as inborn the facts of Kamala and Amala walking on all fours, carrying objects in their mouths, favoring raw meat, howling at night, and, despite being girls, having long hair on their shoulders and chests.

Today, few children on earth face any danger of being thrown into an actual wolf pack. Yet if children acquire ability and develop not by birth but by environment, many of them are more or less as hampered in their development as if they had been thrown among wolves. Furthermore, others view the results of their stunted development, and proclaim the children to have been so "by birth." This is a great error, for the fate of children lies, rather, in the hands of their parents.

– 3 –
What Is Missing from the Environment Will Not Develop on Its Own

The Indeterminacy of a Newborn's Predisposition

Music is what I know best. So, let me discuss in the context of music whether predisposition is innate.

The superiority or inferiority of an individual's natural aptitude has, since long ago, been a topic of discussion. However, people do not determine the presence or absence of natural aptitude by testing newborns. Instead, they wait until children are five or six years old, or even longer, before judging the quality of their propensities by weighing the abilities they have acquired.

Thus, when a child once trumpeted as a prodigy matures into a so-called ordinary person, people conclude that his supposed natural propensity was, from the beginning, not so great. Conversely, when someone who was not particularly noteworthy in her youth later demonstrates staggering ability, people claim the following:

"When it comes to geniuses, there are all kinds. This particular child, in short, belonged to the late-bloomer type."

In other words, when discussing human talent, they merely observe the results of a person's development, link those results to the issue of heredity, then retroactively judge the outcome to reflect innate strengths and weaknesses.

With respect to inborn qualities or hereditary factors, I believe we should only consider the quality of the conditions of a person's physiological functions, since physiological qualities certainly differ from child to child already at the time of birth. When it comes to establishing the quality of an infant's cultural ability, however, it is impossible to discern at birth.

This is because, within that very early, very brief period between birth and the next two or three years, a child absorbs everything from her environment and creates the core of her abilities in response to the given conditions of her environment. Adults have no way of verbally instructing the child in this process, nor does she attempt consciously to learn from the environment.

Rejecting the Thought of Specific Natural Traits

I hope this point makes sense based on the examples of Kiuchi Hiromi and the fledgling bushwarblers. The quality of our environments powerfully acts to shape the quality of our abilities. All the more so, then, that supposedly innate gifts and defects are impossible to measure once a child has reached five or six years of age.

It seems to me to be terribly futile to argue about something that we have no way of measuring, and to ascribe results to it. Instead, from my years of experience as a music educator working with young children, I have come to a point where I am no longer able to accept the existence of specific natal traits such as musical ability. To have the capacity to develop tone deafness or even to become a wolf—this I believe is precisely the essential character of human beings.

Rather than being generated from within as a result of heredity, I propose that all cultural abilities develop within while adapting to external environmental conditions. When it comes to hereditary human superiority or inferiority, observed differences stem from nothing other than variety in the quality of ability acquisition and formation; in other words, the sensitivity and speed with which humans adapt to their environments. Accordingly, being born with superior natal traits means one possesses outstanding sensitivity and speed for adapting to the environment.

To be able to adapt to a wolf's sensibility and habits is indeed the very essence of human nature. Thus, be it Einstein, Goethe, or Beethoven, had he been born in the Stone Age he would have attained no greater cultural ability than that of the people of that age. The same can be said of the reverse. If I were to receive a Stone Age baby under my tutelage, I would raise him to become a youth who plays Beethoven violin sonatas. Again, if a baby born today were to be reared in a society five thousand years from now, he would surely adapt to the circumstances of that society.

What Is Missing from the Environment Will Not Develop on Its Own

The potential of human children is as I described above. Therefore, children born in the nations of the West, the East, and Africa develop in response to the different cultures of their nations and regions. Today once again, I keenly feel that in each of these areas, humans of infinite variety are developing while adapting to parents and environments of infinite variety.

Without causes, there are no results. This is true in all matters. Indications of failed or successful upbringing, a beautiful or twisted heart, superior or inferior sensitivity—these represent the development that the life forces of children have achieved while adapting to their environments.

A certain Dr. Pronko of the Department of Psychology at Wichita State University, Kansas, visited me in Matsumoto four years ago. He has studied these matters empirically and published his findings in American academic circles as follows:

"On raising a large number of infants for nine months following birth in a variety of cultural environments, it was found that their abilities developed in response to those respective environments, and that what is missing from the environment will not develop on its own."

I would like, here, to repeat my appeal: we must stop taking a developed form for something innate. Let's take into consideration the unknown, yet extremely high, potential with which human children are endowed, realize the fact that innate superiority or inferiority is yet unknowable, and raise them successfully. That, I would suggest, promises true happiness for children and tomorrow's light for humankind.

Will He Amount to Anything? No, He Won't Be a Thing

One day, the mother of one of my students stopped by to see me. Her son was an excellent student who practiced well and had developed a fine musical sense. "Mr. Suzuki, will my child amount to anything?" I laughed as I answered her question: "No, ma'am, he won't be a *thing*."

It is a current trend among many parents to hold this sort of view. But to me it starkly reveals the calculating educational attitude that they are allowing their children to try the violin only if the children might turn out to be special, and this always compels me to respond in jest as in the above. The mother looked surprised by my answer, and so I elaborated:

"But your child will be a fine human being. That's sufficient, isn't it? I'd recommend avoiding the implication that it's not worth the effort unless he's particularly gifted, and that you'll have him give up the training otherwise. It feels to me when parents question whether a child will amount to anything, that behind the question lurks an unwholesome view of the child as potentially a *usable thing*, or worse, a *profitable thing*.

"I prefer to think that a parent nurturing a child should be satisfied with helping the child develop, to whatever degree possible, toward becoming an accomplished and beautiful-hearted person, and to head toward a path of happiness. If the child develops respectably as a human being, a respectable path will open up for him. On the other hand, if the parent makes him hopeless as a human being, the child has no choice but to walk along a hopeless path.

"Your child's violin playing is developing wonderfully. Let's you and I together continue our efforts to refine his heart."

A Youth Who Learned the Basics from His Father

"I'd like to entrust you with my child."

This was what Etō Toshiya's father had said 30-odd years ago when he brought his four-year-old son to me. It was with these words that Toshiya became my very first child student. Three or four years later, the father of Toyoda Kōji, another of my young students, moved his family from Hamamatsu to Tokyo when I moved there from Nagoya.

When engaged in the fostering of children, one comes to know different types of parents. Mr. Y of the Nagoya chapter, whom I had instructed in the violin long ago, asked me one day, "Would you kindly listen sometime to my son's violin playing?"

I learned that his 18-year-old son, whom he taught, was now playing Mozart's *Concerto No. 5*.

"With pleasure," I replied. "Please send him to Matsumoto any time."

About a month later, his son visited me at home on his own. It was the first time I was meeting the youth, and it struck me that his voice and Nagoya dialect-inflected speech patterns were nearly identical to those of his father. The way he clasped his hands while greeting me, and the way he laughed, were so like his father that I almost had the illusion that I was indeed talking with Mr. Y.

Impressed by how well he took after his father, I prompted him to play his violin. He pulled his violin out of its case and began tuning it. The busy movements of his bow as he tuned were again exactly like his father's. It was too soon to be surprised, however.

If You See the Parent, You Know the Child

When the son began playing, he was the spitting image of Mr. Y not only in his posture and bow-hand movements, but in very subtle areas including the strengths and weaknesses of his performance, his musical sensitivity, the occasionally flawed intonation, and his tone color.

Never did I more vividly feel than in that moment the presence of a human child whose development reflects an adaptation to his environment. The fact that this youth grew for 18 years in the same home as his father was incontrovertibly demonstrated in his heart, sensibilities, behavior—everything. It revealed the wondrous power spun together by a single life force.

At some point the three-year-old Toyoda Kōji was playing "Humoresque" while seven-year-old Etō Toshiya was learning a concerto. A certain father who had seen them perform brought his three-year-old son to me and asked, "May I request an appraisal as to whether this child of mine has any musical predisposition . . . "

In other words, he intended to let the boy take lessons if he was talented. How could one possibly appraise the level of musical or literary talent in a three year old? Despite my best efforts, I was unable to make the father understand my explanation that talent is not innate but must be developed. Moreover, such parents abound in society.

Observing the innumerable ways in which Mr. Y's son was turning out exactly like his father, I thought to myself, "When it comes to the matter of a child's aptitude, an appraisal of the parents would seem to be the wiser path to a rough guess."

– 4 –
The Amazing Workings of the Life Force

The Bow Jumps; the Mother Retrieves It

All branch chapters of Talent Education throughout the country accept every child without any admissions tests. This is because we operate on the assumption that talent is not inborn, and that every child develops in proportion to her life experience and the efforts she expends.

"Let's have children study the violin as a way to acquire a beautiful heart, artful sensibility, and refined abilities. The violin is the medium through which we cultivate their humanity."

Teachers of every branch chapter operate on this principle. They collaborate with the parents of their students in a joint effort to foster something precious in each child, who in effect constitutes life itself. Among those efforts undertaken by our teachers is the following example.

This took place in the Nakatsugawa city chapter of Gifu prefecture. Among the many children at this studio was a six-year-old girl who had contracted polio. The right side of her body was severely affected, and her right eye was unable to focus. When she played the "Twinkle" rhythm "takataka tatta," her right hand moved abruptly of its own accord with each "tatta," whereupon her bow would fly out of her hand.

Her teacher, Yogo Ninzaburō, was at a loss as to how to surmount this challenge, and consulted with me. My answer at the time was brief.

"Let's continue with this student until both teacher and parent give up."

Instructor Yogo pulled himself together and patiently continued with the girl's lessons. I have no doubt that it must have been very hard on the mother, whose role it was to pick up the bow that flew out of her child's hand each time she played "tatta."

Finally, however, there came a time when the instructor and mother's great love and effort won out. The movements of the child's right hand gradually changed, until in the end the girl's bow stopped leaping out of her hand when she played "tatta."

An Indefatigable Half Year Later

Eventually, a half year later, this child was able to play the "Twinkle Variations." Thanks to her daily training during that period, her right arm grew stronger and she acquired the capacity to maneuver her bow. These developments were the result of an awe-inspiring endeavor that brought together as one the child, mother, and teacher. What had once seemed impossible became possible over the course of their efforts. An ability was thus created that would have wound up nonexistent had they given up. Invisible, tiny amounts of accumulated ability bred yet more ability and finally blossomed into a substantial ability.

When I congratulated the mother on her tremendous efforts, she replied:

"Yes, I wished to help my daughter in any way I could to enable her to play this one piece, if nothing else. Her bow fell to the floor so often that on occasion I even tied it to her bow arm . . . But she can now play the piece, and is as delighted as I am . . . "

However, the daughter's achievement did not end solely with learning that one piece. Thankfully, as she continued practicing the violin, her right eye gradually learned to focus properly, and at the same time the entire right side of her body, until then debilitated, began to move like everyone else's.

The girl thus overcame her handicap. Unexpectedly, she was restored to complete physical health. In other words, the efforts she and her mother invested toward mastering a single piece of music helped her transcend her bodily limitations.

The Inherent Strengths that Manifest Themselves Through Training

My creed that "ability is life itself" was positively proven before my eyes in a girl stricken with polio. What defines everything in a human being is the power of its life force. The activities of a life force that asserts its will to live reflect the enormous power generated in response to prevailing environmental conditions. Through training alone, a person's vital activities reveal their original nature and create ability. With further continual training, that ability develops into yet higher ability while conquering all difficulties. This, I posit, is the underlying relationship between human beings and their respective abilities.

I discuss elsewhere below how we ought not merely to think but must put our thoughts into practice. At any rate, however, the human spirit demonstrates its power only in those who act, and thus no ability whatsoever will develop in those who neglect to train themselves.

Take for example the girl with polio. Had her parents left her as she was, without encouraging her to do anything because she was ill, she would have resigned herself to her condition and most likely have spent an entire lifetime with the right side of her body disabled.

The challenging physical activities required for playing the violin, and the mental activities required for committing music to memory, activated this child's life force and thereby stimulated it to attain an immense power.

2

Kō and Us

Toyoda Kōji *(left)* **and Dr. Suzuki.**

– 1 –
Wonderful Positive Evidence

A Surprising Letter

In Berlin

Dearest Sensei,

Sensei, I have finally reached this city. I feel a nostalgic pleasure, wondering in which neighborhood of Berlin you might have lived long ago, or asking myself if a particular corner of the city is the one about which I once had a dream. Due to the newness of the buildings in Berlin, there is something rather chilly in its atmosphere, but the people are gracious and polite, unlike in rustic Köln.

On auditioning yesterday, I was given the seat of principal concertmaster for the Berlin Radio Symphony Orchestra. The conductor is Ferenc Fricsay, currently viewed in Germany as being on a par with Herbert von Karajan and Rafael Kubelik.

Right now my only concern is whether I can do justice to such a seat. Please be well.

September 1962

With heartfelt love,

Kōji

So wrote Kōji, who had left for Berlin from Köln (or Cologne, in French), an old city along the middle reaches of the Rhine, in the western part of Germany, known for its perfumes. It was in 1962, when autumn, which comes early in Shinshū, was gradually ripening. I was as pleased as I was astonished.

Blessed with Loving Respect

From the time that Western music first took root in Japan, nobody had ever dreamed that a Japanese musician would one day achieve a position like this. I knew the quality of the Berlin Radio Symphony Orchestra. For a Japanese national—and Kōji, no less—to be its principal concertmaster, the most important position within the orchestra and one that represented all its members . . .

For that position to be bestowed on someone, he or she must demonstrate the following three attributes: first, a refined musical sense; second, outstanding performing ability; and third, commendability as a human being. The young Kōji, although just having turned 30, was recognized to possess these traits. Indeed, it was precisely for this reason that he was selected for the post from among the many European candidates.

Art is the person. The beauty and loftiness of sensibility, heart, and conduct—these constitute the path of those who study and pursue art. This was my belief, and my sole wish for my students was that they would seek out this path.

The footsteps that Kōji trod while single-mindedly applying himself along the main road of art simultaneously followed, as might be expected, a path toward cultivating the image of a human being respected by superior artists. When I read the letters I receive from Yamada Hiroko, who recently became a member of the same orchestra, I realize anew how remarkable a position Kōji holds and I can almost see the way he is loved and respected by the entire orchestra.

Three Dozen Years Ago

I think it quite likely that Kōji loves and respects all human beings, and I also am convinced that within his orchestra his is the most unassuming and kindest human presence. This is something I know to my very core.

Kōji was three years of age when he first performed in one of our student recitals. This particular recital was held at the Japan Youth Hall in Tokyo. At the time Etō Toshiya was seven, and on that day he played a superb rendition of Seitz's *Concerto No. 3* for violin, accompanied by the Tokyo String Orchestra. Five-year-old Arimatsu Yōko gave an accomplished performance, then merrily ran to the wings with her violin on her shoulder. The audience broke into laughter at the endearing sight.

Amidst all this, Kōji, age three and holding a sixteenth-size violin, performed Dvořák's "Humoresque" to the guitar accompaniment of his father. The next morning, a certain leading newspaper hyperbolically wrote this up in its social page under the headline, "A Child Prodigy Appears," with a large photo of Kōji taken while he performed. This was a most regrettable betrayal of what I had repeatedly emphasized to the reporters prior to the recital: "There is no innate talent called genius; genius is an honorific term given to human beings who have been fostered to achieve magnificence." I recall that this episode took place 34 or 35 years ago.

My Precious Friends

Kōji's father lived in Hamamatsu in Shizuoka prefecture. He had studied violin in Nagoya under my instruction. When I moved to Tokyo in the late '20s, he moved his whole family to Tokyo as well. Incredibly, this was all because he wished Kōji to study with me.

In other words, having fun playing the violin was Kōji's life from before he could remember anything. This was wholly aside from any question of whether he liked or disliked the violin. This is precisely the same as the process by which all Japanese children learn Japanese, completely separate from whether or not they like doing so.

Kōji grew up also listening daily to recordings of great musicians. Under these superlative conditions, he had practiced effortlessly and extremely well. Those who practice effectively never fail to acquire consistently masterful performance ability. Thus, even if the three-year-old Kōji played "Humoresque" with unusual skill, that had nothing to do with genius.

Around 1938 or '39, the lesson studio at my home in Tokyo was becoming more and more lively as the number of young students increased. For me, the hours I spent at home giving lessons to these children were an unsurpassed joy. I find great pleasure in having close friends visit me, but these children too are all my precious friends. Now, nearly 30 years later, those youngsters who were at the time my students and friends have matured, each in their own different ways, to become praiseworthy adults, something that gives me a quiet yet deeply felt joy.

My Little Friends All Grown Beautifully

Before long, World War II had started, and I left Tokyo to work at a lumber factory in Kiso-Fukushima in Nagano prefecture, eventually taking up residence in Matsumoto. Since then many years have passed. If I were to investigate more fully, I would come up with many more names, but when I list the students from those days off the top of my head, this is what I remember:

Etō Toshiya (Professor, Curtis Institute of Music; performer)

Arimatsu Yōko (graduate of the Royal Conservatory of Brussels; performer)

Kobayashi Takeshi (Brno Philharmonic Orchestra of Czechoslovakia, concertmaster)

Kobayashi Kenji (graduate of The Juilliard School; performer)

Toyoda Kōji (Berlin Radio Symphony Orchestra, principal concertmaster)

Suzuki Hidetarō (Quebec Symphony Orchestra, concertmaster)

Suwa Nejiko (graduate of the Royal Conservatory of Brussels; performer)

Without exception, every one of my students was accepted into my studio without any kind of screening whatsoever. "Every child develops. Everything depends upon how they are fostered." This was my principle as I guided the development of those lively children, and they have marvelously borne out the claim.

Toshiya, at 11 years of age, placed first at the Mainichi Student Music Competition, and was awarded the Minister of Education Prize. The assigned piece on that occasion was Bach's *Concerto in A Minor*. Kōji, seven years old then, was able to play the same piece with aplomb. I had him perform, too, in order to help the judges realize that Japanese children could achieve this level of proficiency at the tender age of seven. His performance was clearly accomplished enough for him to pass the preliminary screening. I rose, however, and made this request: "The only purpose of Toyoda Kōji's performance today is to have him heard by everyone, so please dispense with any scores for him." At age seven, Kōji had already developed this far.

– 2 –
For Young Kō

To the Kiso-Fukushima Factory by Myself

It was in the 18th year of the Shōwa era, or 1943, when I was just past my mid-forties. Early that year the German forces surrendered in Stalingrad, and in the Pacific, the Japanese forces retreated from Guadalcanal. Following these pivotal events, Japan's situation grew extremely difficult.

At the time, the Suzuki Violin Factory run by my father had been converted as part of the war effort to produce floats for seaplanes. But the Japanese cypress logs essential to the production of those floats were no longer available, so the employees could do little work no matter how ready they were to do their best.

Unless someone entered the mountains of Kiso-Fukushima in Nagano prefecture and cut down more lumber, operations at the factory would come to an end. Learning of this when I visited my father in Nagoya, I decided to go to the mountains.

The timing seemed right for me to make this change. I had a sense that as long as I stayed in Tokyo, my young students were themselves unlikely to move to the countryside as school-aged children were being encouraged to do. Moreover, air raids were certain to target Tokyo. I therefore explained the situation to my students, withdrew from the faculties of both the Teikoku and Kunitachi Music Academies, and presented a letter of resignation to the Mainichi Music Competition, for which I served as a judge. I moved to Kiso-Fukushima alone, took over a traditional clog factory, and promptly retooled it to manufacture float construction materials. No matter what one might say, Japan at the time was in the midst of a national crisis. Although I was totally ignorant of lumber, I had the district forestry office sell me first-rate cypress wood, sawed up the logs as rapidly as possible, and shipped them southwest to Nagoya.

We were able to move at an impressive speed. The work proceeded smoothly at every stage, and the factory in Nagoya finally could move forward with its production of floats. I had always known the joy of living each day to the fullest: to concentrate on whatever task I was given or I faced at the moment, and to do my utmost. This was something that I had learned in my youth from studying the thirteenth-century Zen Master Dōgen and it is something that I continually put into practice. As the months passed, I therefore found my work at the lumber mill as absorbing and pleasant as ever.

Eating Waterweeds to Stave Off Hunger in the Mountains

Nevertheless, the situation deteriorated steadily as the war continued. There was a general food shortage in those days to begin with, but to make matters worse, Kiso-Fukushima, a town in the basin of the upper reaches of the Kiso river, produced no food. As the final stage of war approached, there were no longer any rations. Given that the lumber factory existed to meet the needs of the military, there was a way to acquire food via the black market. I never once bought anything on the black market, however.

My newly-widowed younger sister had moved in with her two children to stay out the war in the countryside. On the factory's days off, we all went into the far depths of the mountains to look for bracken and other wild plants. But anything even barely edible had already been gathered by others, and almost nothing was to be found. We therefore collected waterweeds stuck to the rocks in the river. They were the kind with reddish stems, and we went home with our backpacks stuffed full of them. These we boiled in a big pot with a little salt, but even if the pot nearly overflowed with the freshly picked waterweeds, by the time they had boiled down we were left with no more than half a rice bowl's worth at best.

Even so, it was just slightly better than drinking water, as it almost gave us the feeling that we were eating gruel. We were often reduced to staving off hunger in this manner. I can imagine how hard it was for my sister, whose still-growing children must have had healthy appetites.

Yet there is something profoundly unforgettable about my memories of Kiso-Fukushima, specifically the beauty of the local people's humanity. In particular the Michishita family, from whom we rented rooms along with an old man called Nakazawa and his family, treated us with genuine warmth and caring. Any time they obtained something good to eat, for example, they always invited us over. Each time we felt restored to life thanks to their hospitality.

Kō, I Am in Kiso-Fukushima

The war became increasingly desperate, but Kiso-Fukushima was a small mountain town completely unscathed by air raids. Every morning in the pure mountain air, the factory employees were good enough to listen attentively to the violin that I played for them for a few minutes before work, by way of what small token of appreciation I could offer as their foreman. Although we experienced considerable distress due to the food shortage, all of us at the factory put our strength together and worked diligently every day to send lumber off to Nagoya.

Then came the end of the war. Around that time I heard through rumor that Kōji's parents had died one after the other. I sent a letter of inquiry in great haste, but Tokyo was a mere remnant of what it had been. Of course there was no reply. Still later I heard from a friend in Tokyo that the orphaned Kōji and his younger brother seemed to have moved elsewhere.

Kōji's father had essentially moved his family to Tokyo to ensure continued violin lessons for his son. Left behind on their own without such devoted parents, I wondered what might have become of the little boys. I could not let the matter rest. I sent a request to the NHK radio broadcast's *Missing People* program asking them to air my inquiry:

"Toyoda Kōji, I am in Kiso-Fukushima. Let me know if you are alive somewhere."

One day about two months later, I received a letter from someone by the name of Toyoda in Hamamatsu, not far from Nagoya. The sender, who turned out to be Kōji's uncle, indicated that he was looking after the boy.

Kōji Becomes a Member of Our Family

"I've found out where Kō-chan is!"[1]

"That's wonderful. How very wonderful. Let's have him over right away."

"We'll send off a letter at once."

As we leaped for joy, this was how the conversation went between my sister and me.

Soon, the 11-year-old Kōji, accompanied by his uncle, arrived at our place of refuge in Kiso-Fukushima. He had grown—yes, it had been three years since I saw him last. My sister and her children, too, were delighted.

Kōji's uncle ran a small shop serving drinks in Hamamatsu.

"Kōji's violin was the last thing on our minds, as I needed his help everyday in the shop."

So saying, the uncle left the boy in our care.

Starting that day, Kōji became a member of our family. And until I sent him abroad to study in Paris at age 19, my sister continued to treat him with a deeply maternal love. His character and conduct are the result of her fostering.

Once Kōji joined us, life at Kiso-Fukushima became a true pleasure. The seven of us occupied two ten-mat rooms[2] on the second floor of the Michishita family's house: my aunt, our housekeeper Okō, the three children, my sister,

---

[1] The author uses the nickname "Kō-chan" to refer to Kōji. "Chan" is a diminutive ending that indicates affection, and is often used with first names and nicknames of children.

[2] In Japan, room sizes are measured in terms of *tatami* mats. The sizes of mats differ regionally, but in central Japan they are typically 0.88 meters wide (2 feet 10 inches) by 1.76 meters long (5 feet 9 inches).

and myself.[3] The seven of us enjoyed passing the evenings together, whatever the activity. Sharing one another's amateur attempts at haiku, for example, provided inexpressible joy and hilarity.

The Entire Family Pulling Together for Kō . . .

But not everything went smoothly.

The three years Kōji spent helping out at his uncle's drinking place in Hamamatsu had completely changed his Tokyo upbringing. An uncouth sensibility and set of behaviors drew our attention. Some members of the family started to complain. What to do?

At any rate, I thought, we can't all start finding fault with him. We needed somehow to avoid scolding him from every direction. One day, therefore, while Kōji was at school, I decided to consult with the adults in the household.

"During the last three years Kō-chan has unconsciously picked up coarse manners and the habit of leaving things unfinished. Still, it would be wrong to scold him now. If we are all chastising him and none of the other children, he's certain to start feeling he's unfairly treated. Let's talk to Yatchan and Mitchan (my sister's children), and propose that we all try, without a word to Kō, to hold ourselves to a higher standard of manners and behavior in our daily lives. I'd like us to create a model environment that allows him to become a well-mannered boy naturally, without even realizing it. I feel that if we simply nag at him, we will inadvertently send him off in a negative direction."

My aunt, my sister Hina, and the housekeeper Okō enthusiastically received my suggestion. And thus, our new lifestyle began the following day: silently, we went about our daily lives with a renewed sense of purpose and attitude of caring.

This is for Kō's sake—with this single thought in mind, we mutually prepared ourselves. It was for Kō's sake; but even more than for him, it turned out to be a fulfilling practice of the heart and conduct for all of us in the family.

---

[3] Around the time that Suzuki moved to Kiso-Fukushima, his wife Waltraud moved to Hakone in Kanagawa prefecture, where many Germans spent the wartime along with other foreign nationals. After the war, Waltraud worked first in Hakone, then in Tokyo, while assisting Suzuki. She rejoined him in Matsumoto in 1956.

In that manner, one year passed and then a second. During that interval, Kōji blended into our daily lives and turned into a truly good boy, not a trace remaining of the scars from the previous three years.

– 3 –
Loftier and More Beautiful

The Inception of the Talent Education Movement

It was 1945, toward the end of our third year at Kiso-Fukushima. Among a circle of Matsumoto residents actively involved with academic and artistic pursuits, a discussion arose about founding a music conservatory in the city. At the center of that talk was the vocalist Mori Tamiki, a colleague of mine from the Teikoku Music Academy, who happened to have evacuated to Matsumoto during the war.

Mr. Mori sent a messenger to my place in Kiso-Fukushima, inviting me to help run the Matsumoto Academy of Music. My answer was guarded, however:

"Back in Tokyo I was engaged often enough in remedial education for students already mistaught to varying degrees, and I must confess I am not keen to take up such endeavors again. My preference would be to pursue early childhood education. I would like in the future to teach small children using the new ideas and methods I have been developing. What I intend is not education for creating prodigies, but rather, a mode of cultivating the abilities of children by means of the violin. Based on my years of study and experimentation, I have confidence that I will be successful with this project, and I therefore would like to devote myself to something of the kind. If I can secure your support for this concept, I am happy to assist along those lines."

Not long thereafter, I heard from Matsumoto that my conditions had been accepted and that they sought my full cooperation. This was how I wound up in Matsumoto, where I eventually settled permanently. During my early days at the academy, I commuted once a week from Kiso-Fukushima. Soon, however, there were too many students to fit into one day a week, and so, welcomed by many kind people, I switched my residence to Matsumoto.

Thus began our Talent Education movement, centered around the Matsumoto Academy of Music.

Kōji, Always Walking with God

As mentioned above, my sister Hina cared unstintingly for Kōji as a mother figure. A heartfelt Catholic, she dedicated her life to the faith, worked for the church as much as possible, was loved by everybody, and did her utmost for my Talent Education movement.

On Sundays Kōji always went to church with my sister. Perhaps due to her great love and influence, he soon became a devout Catholic himself. Again, perhaps thanks to the invisible fostering power of nature, there were striking signs of the development in him of a beautiful heart and remarkable sensibility.

Later on, when Kōji, still an adolescent, was studying music at the Conservatoire de Paris, my sister and I had the following exchange while musing about his being alone in a foreign land:

"It's possible, don't you think," I noted, "that Kō may write to say he wants to study to become a Catholic priest?"

"Yes, I do. For him art and religion seem to be one."

"The odds are very high that he will choose the path of art. But, on the off chance that he writes for permission to enter a theological seminary, let's do grant his wish."

Kōji has since become a fine artist. But as a youth he possessed a strong enough religiosity to cause us to have such a conversation.

The following episode took place when he was about 14. His violin tone had developed a beautiful solidity, and he was already capable of performing with a sensitive, musically nuanced expressivity. One day I made a suggestion.

Aspiring to Be Lofty and Beautiful

After one of his lessons, I told Kōji, who was now able to play Bach's "Chaconne" very well, "Today I would like you to go to the church and play in front of Christ. Play the 'Chaconne' with all your heart for him to hear."

"Yes, sir, I'll be on my way then," he replied, and left immediately with his violin. An hour or so later, he reported back, "I'm home! I played the 'Chaconne' at church."

"Good. How was it?"

"No one else was there, and it felt very comfortable."

"I'm glad. From now on, no matter where or when you play, it will be a good idea always to assume that you are playing for Christ."

"Yes, sir," he replied, his cheerful face brightening even more. He was always a responsive one.

From my life experiences I have come to believe strongly in the importance for young people, including those who may be readers of this volume, to interact with outstanding people. Through doing that, we unconsciously enhance our heart, sensibility, and conduct. Indeed, I think this is a fundamental condition of character building.

Based on this conviction, I chose a pair of teachers for Kōji. They were Professor and Mrs. Sekiya Mitsuhiko, for whom I had great esteem. Professor Sekiya is now on the faculty of International Christian University, but in those days he taught at Shinshū University in Matsumoto.

Requesting of the Sekiyas that they undertake Kōji's further development, I had him commute to their home for various lessons. He initially studied English with Sekiya Ayako, and then later, once we began planning for him to study abroad in France, he received French lessons from Professor Sekiya. I feel deeply grateful that Kōji was able, through his time with them, to be in contact with the couple's gracious, refined ways, and I am certain that his interaction with them has brought him immeasurable happiness in life.

– 4 –
The Moment Had Arrived

Their Amazing Ability

Elsewhere in this book, I will further elaborate on the phenomenon that is human ability, and how it is something to be created rather than genetically acquired. But here, I would like to touch on the same topic more lightheartedly through a story about Kōji.

Kōji and Kobayashi Kenji were very good friends who called each other Ken-chan and Kō-chan with the diminutive ending. The following event took place when they were about 15. Kenji, who lived in Tokyo, happened to come over to Matsumoto with his violin for an extended period of lessons and fun, and the boys had been enjoying themselves for days on end when I received a request for a radio performance from the local NHK affiliate based in Matsumoto.

I considered it an excellent pedagogical opportunity and decided, as a way to evaluate their ability, to have them perform a piece they had never played before—Vivaldi's *Concerto for Two Violins in A Minor*. I was well acquainted with their technical and expressive abilities, but I was curious as to how quickly they could memorize the piece and make it their own.

I informed the radio station of the name of the piece, but spent the following days without telling the boys anything. Then, the morning before the live broadcast, I called them to my room and handed them the sheet music for the concerto.

"You'll be performing all three movements of this piece on the radio tomorrow afternoon at one o'clock. I know this is sudden, but it will be good training for you. Today you'll want to start practicing this right away."

Exclaiming to each other, "Uh, oh, we're in trouble now," and "We'd better get serious," they delightedly ran to their room, each with his assigned part.

It wasn't long before I started to hear the sound of the *Concerto for Two Violins*. After about an hour and a half, I peeked into their room upstairs, wanting to make a few suggestions concerning musical expressivity in their performance of the piece. I found them already playing the first movement together without referring to the sheet music. It was a marvel.

To the Radio Station, Leaving the Music Behind at Home

I went out on business, leaving the boys while they practiced away. Later, with all the members of the household gathered for dinner, I asked them, "How are things coming along? Does it seem like you'll be ready in time?"

One of the boys responded, "You really pulled one on us today," while the other noted, "Still, though, it's a good piece."

Despite their talk of having run into a tough challenge, they looked extremely happy and gave off not a whiff of anxiety.

On the following day, before they went to the station, I asked to hear their duo. Before they started playing, they first handed me the printed music. I placed it on my desk, and listened. Handing the music to me before they play is a custom by which my young students have always abided.

When they finished playing, I told them, "Very well played. Your tone and expressivity were both stellar. You'll do fine. Now go and perform your best. I'll be listening to your performance from home."

The station had sent a car for the two of them, and as they climbed in, they called out, "We'll be back soon!" in high spirits. Naturally, their music still laid on my desk. As I will write below, developing the capacity to memorize is one of the pedagogical areas in which I place the greatest emphasis. The printed music is nothing but a reference for memorization. It never even occurred to Kōji and Kenji, who had grown up with this assumption, to bring the music with them to the recording studio.

The Time Had Come to Find Kōji a Master Teacher

Ability develops to the degree that it is fostered, I reflected afresh after sending the boys off to the station. They had left without an ounce of concern, having perfectly committed to memory all the movements of a concerto they had learned only the day before, on top of which they were to play not in unison but as an ensemble . . .

My test was over. Their performance on air was truly exemplary. Listening to it with my family, I was brimming with joy and emotion. I wonder if the two of them, now accomplished musicians, ever recall that occasion.

Of course, I screened neither boy when I originally welcomed them into my studio. Nor do I consider their magnificent skills and powerful ability as things to be attained only by exceptional people, an attitude of mine that has been reinforced by experience. Students who are fostered thusly develop thusly—the cases of Kōji and Kenji are no more than illustrations of this belief.

Eventually, Kōji turned 19 as a member of our family. The time had come for me to think about finding a preeminent teacher for him and for his artistic development. My choice was Georges Enescu (1881–1955) of Romania, the consummate twentieth-century artist and violinist.

What on Earth Is This About?

Enescu was of an advanced age by then, but knowing that he was still in Paris, I was determined to send Kōji to Paris to study with him, and to learn from his tremendous character and supreme artistry.

Three years before Enescu's death, that is to say in November 1952, I received a letter from Paris from Kōji, conveying the following news:

> I have successfully tested for entrance into the Conservatoire de Paris, and will be studying with Professor Benedetti. My friends have informed me that Maestro Enescu is ill and does not take students . . .

I wrote back, chagrined.

> What on earth is this about? Did you not cross the sea to Paris in order to study with Maestro Enescu? Why then did you simply inquire with your friends and neglect even to pay him a visit?
>
> If you have learned that Maestro Enescu is ill, is that not all the more reason to visit and inquire after his health? Even simply to tell him that you have come from Japan out of admiration for him and in order to study with him—that is the very least you ought to do for the maestro you hold in esteem. This is entirely separate from whether or not you are able to take lessons from him.

After a while I received a delightful letter from Kōji. Full of emotion, it conveyed something along the following lines.

– 5 –
Becoming Grumiaux's Prized Student

Kōji's Affecting Letter

Sensei,

Reading your letter, I thought it was just so. I immediately looked up Maestro Enescu's address and visited him without a moment's delay.

He was kind enough to meet with me. He is a wonderfully distinguished person. It is true that he is somewhat fragile from age. However, he generously invited me to play something for him.

I decided to play Bach's "Chaconne." When I finished, he told me,

"I would be pleased to have you come to my home to study with me. But you are now Professor Benedetti's student. I cannot be so rude as to take his student away from him. Instead, come to me when you graduate from the Conservatoire."

Sensei, I will make every effort to graduate as quickly as possible.

I wrote back to Kōji in the following vein.

Celebrating His Blessings

Dear Kōji,

Thank you for your letter.

How lovely that you visited Maestro Enescu. From here on I believe you will become even more personally aware of the fact that being in contact with magnificent examples of humanity—and even better with towering figures mentally and physically purified through art—is the greatest happiness on earth.

And how much you can perceive that greatness and beauty will contribute to your human worth. I should note, however, that the capacity to perceive and acquire can only be created by lowering yourself, gazing at the true value of this earth's phenomena, and thereby accumulating truth, love, and knowledge.

You are now at Maestro Enescu's side. This fact gives me the greatest peace of mind and joy. If I were allowed to wish further, how wonderful it would be for you to cross paths on a regular basis with one other person, Dr. Albert Schweitzer.

Nevertheless, under no circumstances does the act of perceiving what is superior emanate from that object. One must possess within oneself that ability to perceive. In order to acquire something lofty, one must develop one's inner ability to yet more powerful levels. Only those who are successful at that are able to experience the joy of being in the proximity of superior individuals.

To do that one must always be humble—for an arrogant heart loses its ability to know truth and greatness. Please do not lose sight of this fact.

Half a year later, graduation examinations took place at the Conservatoire.

Graduating from the Conservatoire de Paris in Half a Year

A half year after his entrance, Kōji was already participating in the graduation exams. It was an astounding development. Kōji had impressively managed to graduate from the Conservatoire following a mere half year of enrollment.

A diploma from the Conservatoire de Paris—it must be a great joy for anyone. In Kōji's case, however, to receive it meant the particular joy of now being able to study with Maestro Enescu.

Kōji was thus formally able to become the maestro's student within months of first visiting him. Kōji subsequently received his instruction for two years, until this maestro passed away. How many invaluable teachings Kōji must have received and absorbed during those two years. I believe that the scope of what he learned in that time surpasses the imagination.

By the time he lost Maestro Enescu, however, Kōji had developed into a youth capable of seeking out his own teacher. It was Arthur Grumiaux whom he chose. Grumiaux is a professor of the Royal Academy of Music in Brussels, an illustrious master who is actively engaged both on the concert stage and in recording studios, and who is recognized today as the leading violinist in Europe. Kōji was deeply moved by Grumiaux's brilliant performances, and had set his heart on studying with him.

Currently Grumiaux has two students whom he cherishes as his best. Both of these students are Japanese, and both studied with me from early on.

Needless to say, one of them is Toyoda Kōji. The other is Shida Tomiko, who began studying with Grumiaux after Kōji, and who won first prize at the ARD International Music Competition in Munich in 1963.

Professor Grumiaux, Kōji's and Tomiko's Teacher

It must have been four years ago that Grumiaux came to Japan accompanied by his wife. He was on a concert tour sponsored by the Osaka International Festival. On that occasion, it was Grumiaux himself who expressed a wish to visit Matsumoto. I thus met Kōji's and Tomiko's teacher for the first time, and, in addition to witnessing his splendid artistry in recital, was able to confirm for myself his majestically humane, noble character, all of which made me feel inordinately blessed.

An outstanding individual, to my mind, is an unpretentious person with a warm heart, lofty spirit, and unadorned, human simplicity. Kōji's and Tomiko's teacher, too, was someone who compelled me to feel what I always feel in the presence of remarkable individuals, whether Japanese or foreign. I was awash with contentment and gratitude for Kōji and Tomiko.

Shida Tomiko's playing, too, is truly exquisite. She had already been cultivating the beautiful heart and unerring musical sense that are absolutely indispensible to reaching a high level of artistry, but under the instruction of a great teacher like Grumiaux she was further polishing her abilities. I now consider it a matter of course that she, having acquired such invaluable qualities, placed first at the competition in Munich.

I suppose it must been seven or eight years ago when the following episode involving Shida Tomiko took place.

Simply Dedicate Your Performance to Chausson's Soul

Every year in Matsumoto, we hold a Talent Education summer school. About a thousand people gather from all over Japan to enjoy studying music together. And every evening during the institute we organize a wonderful concert.

One year, before she had gone away to Europe, Shida Tomiko was to perform "La Poème" by Ernest Chausson (1855–1899) at one of those evening concerts. However, during our ride together in a car headed for the hall, Tomiko told me, "Sensei, this piece is so difficult, I'm feeling a little nervous." "What is it that's worrying you," I prompted her.

"Are you playing that marvelous piece for the audience? Your performance is not some kind of merchandise to put on display, you know. Don't think of it as a show for an audience. It's fine to make mistakes. If you flub something, you can play it again. Tonight, I want you to play that divine piece before the spirit of the composer. Face to face with Chausson's wonderfully poetic soul and his depth of emotion, see if you can communicate back your own emotional response. If you do that, there is nothing to worry about. You will be in a world where there is nobody and nothing except you and Chausson."

Shida's performance that night was profoundly stirring. Moved to tears, I sprang up on stage and clasped her hand with heartfelt blessings. This young woman, who in later years was to become one of Grumiaux's prized students, had attained a memorable level of expressivity in the process of receptively taking in my heart and words, then playing before Chausson's spirit with emotional depth and conviction.

3

A Path Toward the Extraordinary

A lesson with young students.

– 1 –
The Folly of Lamenting a Lack of Talent

To Give Up Is to Know Oneself

I spent nearly all of my twenties overseas, studying in Berlin. On my arrival in Germany, I searched for a violin teacher whom I could believe to be the best, and found Professor Karl Klingler. His assignments were so difficult, however, that no matter how hard I tried, even when I went to such lengths as practicing five hours daily, they blocked my advance like a colossal wall. This state of affairs continued for days and months on end. I made no progress at all. Then came forlorn resignation.

"There's no hoping otherwise; I have no talent to speak of."

On top of this, the performances of the great maestros dealt me one blow after another, as if to taunt me. On those evenings when I made my way home after being enthralled by the brilliant performances delivered at the Berlin Philharmonic concert hall, I felt my own incompetence piercing me to the marrow of my bones.

"How pathetic! My talent can only be described as feeble, and yet I slog away at this day after day. What value can there possibly be in these efforts that will take me nowhere? I just don't have the kind of talent that wells up from within. To give up now may well mean to know myself."

Utterly dejected, I began reasoning thus to myself.

This sort of thing can occur to anyone in their youth, to some degree or other, and often more than once. Especially those who pursue artistic paths experience it almost without exception. It is the natural grief and despair into which people fall when, having been taught that "ability is innate," they come into contact with the tremendous ability of their predecessors, as revealed in their magnificent works of art, and compare it with their own.

Even If One Has No Talent

Sadly, it is not uncommon for youths to despair of their perceived lack of talent and to end up taking their own lives. Even if they do not go to that extent, they are likely to begin a life of mournful resignation, devoid of hope. If only they knew that talent is not something one has, but rather is something one must create, they would surely embark, before lamenting their lack of ability, on a life-long path of hopeful, if daunting, efforts to acquire talent.

From the time I left Japan, my purpose was in fact not to become a performer. Deeply drawn to music, I wished to know the secret behind the human creation of art, or stated differently, "What is art?" Despite my being, or rather because I was, despondent about my capacity as a performer, I was spurred to pursue with even greater determination the secret to art. Indeed, that pursuit is what rescued me from wallowing inconsolably for too long.

Even if I had no talent, I would have to cultivate myself step by step, however slow my pace, in order to construct an interior life suited to a human being. I could not possibly abandon that effort. It was in this way that my heartfelt desire for the pursuit of art saved me from extreme despair.

I did not rush myself. Yet I did not rest, either. Instead, I tirelessly continued my efforts, which gave me both encouragement and peace of mind.

Realizing the Folly of Lamenting One's Lack of Ability

Thanks to this diligence, I began to notice signs of ability—perhaps not a glorious ability, but ability nonetheless—developing in me.

"I have no talent to speak of."

I now recognize how worthless and absurd such worries and sorrows are. It is a false idea that was implanted in all of humanity at some point in our collective murky past, having served since then as a convenient excuse for those who wished to avoid or neglect hard work.

Today, I am confidently able to state, "Human beings are begotten by their environment." If only I had realized this during those difficult years of training long ago in my past, I would surely have trodden a more appropriate path in fostering my ability.

"Every child is capable of development; everything hinges on the way the child is brought up. Each of us is also equipped to develop ourselves, although in this case as well everything depends on the proper effort we devote to the process."

Cowardice: Giving Up on the Pretext of Deficient Talent

Poor talent is the result of misguided effort. Conversely, superior talent is the result of an accumulation of diligently implemented, effectively carried out efforts. It is my wish that readers particularly attend to this point. As for what constitutes a diligent and effective approach, that is something I will explain later. Here, I will simply ask you to keep in mind a single idea: the concept of repetition. If you have learned to do something, be sure to repeat it thoroughly.

Science, as a field, confirms the unknown as unknown. That being the case, people who even bring up the question of science need to stop characterizing human ability, which is one of the unknowns, as "innate." We must each of us also refrain from being superstitious about the development of our own ability. By far the worst, however, is to give up on our own efforts based on the pretext of an absence or presence of talent; this can only be called an act of cowardice.

– 2 –
See the Reality for Yourself

Clumsiness Stems from Flawed Training

One day during the years I taught at Teikoku Music Academy, a female student complained to me.

"Sensei, I'm just too clumsy! My fingers simply refuse to move quickly."

"Clumsy? Who decided that?" I asked. We then had the following exchange:

"It's how I feel."

"You misjudge yourself then. You're telling yourself that you're clumsy. It's no different than applying the brakes, then groaning that your car won't run."

"But my fingers don't move quickly enough."

"Are they injured? Oh, they're not? In that case, place your left hand on the desk. Now, I want you to imitate me, as if you're playing the piano with your fingertips. Try moving your fingers quickly like I'm doing. Aha, you see how quickly your fingers are moving!

"Listen to me now. The problem is not with your fingers, but rather is in your head. There's a disconnection between the operation of your fingers and your brain. Your fingers and brain haven't been trained to work together. This means that your practice methods themselves are at fault. In other words, your efforts are taking you in the wrong direction."

"What should I do then?"

"When I was your age, I too threw myself wholeheartedly into ineffective practice methods. There was no one to teach me to practice differently. So try this. Starting today, I want you to take that fast passage and practice it slowly and carefully, over and over again, for three days. On the fourth day, speed things up a little and keep it at that for two days. Then, on the sixth day, try playing it up to tempo."

The student practiced according to my instructions. At her lesson the following week, she was able to perform the piece without a hitch at the expected speed.

A Joy Shared by 30 Workers

At one point I was invited to lecture at a large factory where fairly detailed handiwork was required of workers on the production line. After the lecture, the company president consulted with me in passing.

"We have about 30 workers who are slow with their hands. All of them work hard, but of course they can't overcome their inborn slowness. We end up taking a loss on them, and at the moment I'm in the red. I'm wondering if there's any chance Talent Education can help?"

A recollection of the female student flashed before me.

"You mentioned the slowness of your employee's hands just now, but I can tell you it is actually a matter of slow minds rather than slow hands."

"Wait, it's not their hands? Then . . . "

"Then there's no way out of the problem," the president was about to say. I interrupted by suggesting that he require those 30 workers to quit work one hour early each day, and to have them spend that hour on intensive ping pong training sessions in the factory's ping pong room.

"Please find a good coach for them," I continued. "Ping pong requires instant, coordinated responses of the mind and body, so when your employees develop proficiency at ping pong, their efficiency on the job should also increase."

"An interesting approach," the company president replied. "We'll give it a try." About half a year later, I received a delightful thank-you note:

"Thanks to your recommendation, the workers have all become skilled ping pong players. Just as you said, their efficiency on the production line has improved in tandem with the progress they've made at playing ping pong. Naturally, we too are happy, but even greater is the joy of the employees who are now able to achieve better-than-average work results while also enjoying ping pong. It is truly something to behold."

Young Hiroko, Super Slow at Everything

I myself was 17 or 18 when I started learning the violin. Adapting to the living conditions under which I grew up, the little finger on my left hand had developed with no capacity at all for playing the violin. It would not respond when I tried to move it quickly, nor did it have the power necessary to press the strings down. It therefore revealed a truly pitiable lack of ability, especially when trilling.

I cannot even count the number of months and years I spent training daily so as to cultivate in this finger an ability and responsiveness close to those of my other fingers. Even now, after over 40 years, I feel that it has never yet been able to catch up with those other fingers. This is the constant struggle faced by those of us who miss out on the optimal period for developing a particular ability.

As a result of having experienced this painful truth myself, I attempted, with my students who started learning the violin at age four or five, to train the little finger on their left hand to move like their other fingers. In so doing, I discovered that their little fingers easily developed such dexterity that it made me, their instructor, envious.

When one's senses, physical movements, or other abilities are trained during this period of abundant flexibility, they will smoothly attain new levels of performance while adapting to any and all conditions in the child's environment.

One of my students was a six-year-old by the name of Hiroko. She grew up in a remote area of Manchuria, but she and her family were repatriated to Japan after World War II. Her grandmother, having heard one of my lectures, brought her to the Matsumoto Academy of Music. Perhaps not unexpectedly for a child from the depths of a frontier colony, Hiroko herself was supremely unhurried in her every movement. No matter what she did, she lagged far behind the other children. I therefore came up with a plan for her.

Amazing Changes After a Dozen Years

Picture the second floor of the Academy. Lining up several children of about the same age as Hiroko, I stand before them. "Get set!" I call out. "One, two ... three!" With that, I bring my right hand to the top of my head as swiftly as I can. The children follow suit. This is training for intuitively catching the moment I call out, "Three!" and for responding with a quick, sudden motion. These two skills are essential to mastering the violin.

Children thoroughly enjoy games of this kind. My students were particularly carried away by this game, which I always introduced before the start of lessons, and they would giggle delightedly. In contrast, however, Hiroko leisurely brought her hand to her head. It was as if time did not exist for her.

Oblivious to the fact that I was trying to teach her to move instantaneously as a prerequisite to learning the violin, Hiroko moved her hand at a snail's pace. I, however, continued to incorporate this hand-to-head game at each lesson, playing as earnestly as the other, more agile children. Even after Hiroko eventually came to play the violin well, I did my utmost to develop in her an acute intuition and dexterity of movement.

Twelve or thirteen years passed, and finally some amazing changes occurred. In the process, Hiroko became the most technically proficient, and immensely memorable, performer in the academy.

A Japanese woman currently resides in Berlin as a member of the Berlin Radio Symphony Orchestra. That woman is little Hiroko of yore—Yamada Hiroko, to be exact.

Ten Years of Effort Can Turn the Inferior into the Exceptional

People often neglect a child's shortcomings as "inborn." However, it is absolutely within the realm of possibility to transform those deficiencies into strengths if one commits to a 10-year plan to train the child. Anyone can develop their abilities, given 10 years of unceasing efforts toward such a goal; I firmly believe this to be true. Indeed, even if it is for no more than a year, if someone is able continually to strive to attain that goal, they can turn flaws into strengths. If a person subsequently continues with those efforts for 10 years, she will become extraordinary. That is because the process of such training stimulates one's life force to activate its tremendous potential.

All humans have their unique shortcomings. The one most commonly seen is to put off something that one knows ought to be done. To put one's thoughts into immediate action is a crucial ability that will have bearing on a person's entire life. Furthermore, like other abilities, it can only be gained through much practice. This ability, in turn, will contribute towards the development of one's desired talents.

Additionally, if you put your principles into practice but last no more than three days, you cannot expect to accomplish anything. When your life force dictates you to think, "I want to do this," you must keep at it until you create the ability finally to accomplish whatever it is, otherwise you will go nowhere.

We all have unlimited shortcomings. Yet one way of seeing things is to consider our lives as a time frame that allows us continually to work at changing our weaknesses into strengths. This, I must say, is an intriguing task. It is as exciting as watching a horse that initially trails behind a number of other horses but passes them one by one and finishes in the lead.

– 3 –
Repeat, and Repeat Again

The Ninja Art of Leaping

Let me share a few more ideas about how to cultivate one's own ability.

I once read about the training methods involved in *ninjutsu*, or the art of concealment and attack employed by *ninja* spies and assassins in feudal Japan. Among them was a method for learning how to leap high: "Sow hemp seeds, raise them, and jump over the shoots every day." I felt that this method, as an approach to developing extraordinary ability, contained a truth worthy of reflection. It addresses the following issues:

> Hemp grows quickly. But the growth is imperceptible to someone looking at it every day. Nevertheless, hemp grows ceaselessly, minute by minute. If one jumps over the hemp daily without rest, even as one remains unaware of the plant's growth, one's leaping ability likewise develops day by day.

If you suddenly look again at the hemp after one or two months, it will have grown to an astonishing height. If you suddenly try to jump over it without having fostered your ability to leap in the weeks prior to that, there is no way you can do it. Conversely, however, if you have worked hard during the hemp's growth period, you will easily and naturally accomplish the feat. To witness someone else succeed, then lament your innate lack of ability, is nothing more than self-serving egotism.

We speak Japanese with freedom, which is in fact a spectacular achievement. What this means is that we all acquire the ability to speak using the same training approach a *ninja* might have used by jumping daily over a hemp plant from the time it first sprouted. Stated differently, an activity will feel easy if the ability for it has been nurtured. Repeat something until it is easy—herein lies the secret of developing your own talents.

Look at Your Right Hand

Who is it that develops your ability? Ability does not develop innately. It is up to you. Each one of us is responsible for developing our own selves. Don't lament your lack of ability without trying to cultivate that ability.

Your left hand is far inferior to your right hand if you have allowed it to stay idle. Even though they both belong to you, your left and right hands reveal a tremendous difference between the one that receives training in the form of every day use, and the one that does not. This applies as well to your ability as a human being. It is folly to consider a talent innately flawed when you have done nothing to develop it.

Look, now, at your right hand. If you train yourself daily the way you have trained your dominant hand, strength will be generated, sensitivity will be fostered, and ability will gradually develop.

The ability possessed by your right hand, which surpasses your left, was not created by someone else. You have created it yourself. When you were born, neither hand was superior or inferior. Why then do they function so differently?

No ability is ever demonstrated innately. Indeed, ability is created only when you make efforts to develop it. Your right hand, for one, knows that you yourself are the creator of your abilities.

How, then, did the extraordinary ability of your right hand come into being? It must have developed through repetition. To become an exceptional human being requires the same approach. If you neglect a talent you have acquired, it will not improve. Repeat what you have achieved to ensure that you can still succeed at it, try it once again with even better results, and further repeat it with yet more impressive results . . . It is only by reinforcing your skills that you will see continual improvement.

The extraordinary originates there, resulting in far superior achievements than those in other people, like the right hand in comparison to the left.

The Ineffable Strength of Heartfelt Repetition

Toil away for your own sake.

Common sense is flawed in its assumption that something already inherent to a person acts on its own to enable that person to achieve anything. Rather, if there is any particular skill you can perform with ease, that is unalloyed proof that you have acquired the ability required to carry out that skill, that it has become part of you.

Something becomes part of you—this is achieved by repeating one's efforts until a particular skill is absorbed, and then further continuing to repeat it.

The above passages serve as admonishment for myself. They represent an awareness that I reached during my years of study in Germany, once I had grappled with my initial despair over the inadequacy of my performance abilities. I think this is an extremely important awareness for my young readers—and, for that matter, for older people as well. Even now, decades later, I perpetually strive not to forget this epiphany. As an example of my attempts to remain conscious of it, I recently wrote with brush and ink the following motto of mine on 1,500 poetry cards:

"Sound breathes life—
  Without form it lives."

The calligraphy was meant as a gift to our little graduates. I rise early every morning, stealing a few minutes from slumber to write a few more cards. Some people comment that it must be hard work. However, far from finding it hard, I take great pleasure in it. As long as I am going to write, I wish to write well. I therefore rub an inkstone with care in my inkwell, and write the same words, card by card, while exhorting myself to write better with each one.

Not being a calligrapher of any sort, writing with a brush is difficult for me. Still, I gain new confidence with each card, my writing becoming more imbued with life, and my calligraphy gradually improving in its own limited fashion. No one card is the same as any other. In this way, I savor the ineffable taste of repetition.

What It Means to Be Capable of Doing Everything

The lesson I formulated for myself has, unaltered, also become the method of Talent Education. In essence, it is the result of my attempts to redesign my flawed practice methods and other efforts of the past into a more productive approach.

When students have learned a piece, all too often they immediately move on to the next piece, and the next. Having played this and that, they claim to have mastered such and such number of pieces. They come to be able to play everything more or less acceptably, except that they don't have a single piece at which they excel.

When they continue to work in this manner for a number of years, they come to a point where they can only give hopeless, mediocre performances. They claim to be able to play anything and everything, but in reality they have come to a halt with many shortcomings still unaddressed.

This problem is not limited to music; it is the case in any arena. In other words, the general rule for becoming accomplished at something is to build up to the highest possible point the strength one has already fostered.

I require my students to practice intensively their most recent piece: they are to play it three times daily for three months or so. At the same time, I assign them to listen constantly to the most exquisite recording in the world of that piece, so that they aspire to play it better and better.

This approach eventually generates results on a higher plane. It is no longer a matter of technique but enters the realm of the spirit. The spiritual attitude of a person while playing the violin, as well as in the moments afterwards—this is a crucial matter of temporal space, known as *ma* in Japanese. When the piece ends, the music has not ended yet. J. S. Bach indicated this by inserting fermatas (⌢)—a symbol denoting the extension of a note or a rest—into his compositions, using early eighteenth-century ink. This pause or elongation corresponds to the vital moment and attitude of stillness in a person who quietly remains kneeling at the end of a prayer. That is the realm to which one must ascend. It is my observation that the technique, sensibility and heart of those who have been able to climb to that height in a musical composition already eclipse that of others who have not yet reached that state.

– 4 –
Neither Make Haste, Nor Dawdle

Perseverance: A Crucial Element of Achievement

As I have stated above, ability is something you create yourself. It is also acquired through repeated practice. The question then becomes the perseverance required to follow through on a task.

"I'm going to persist at this, come what may"—countless people make such resolutions at the outset of an endeavor. Anyone can make a resolution, of course, but in truth, very few of them persist to the end. We tend to make a resolution but fail to carry it out, or, even if we carry it out, we quit before long. Indeed, many people know this well from personal experience. In any undertaking, the path to success, or failure, can be said to hinge on the sole question of whether or not one persists at it. In other words, such perseverance is also something one must cultivate, because it too is an ability. How to do this, then? If you embark on something with resolution, then you need to prepare to endure for a while.

Flog yourself into wakefulness, for this initial perseverance determines your fate. This is because when you endure the challenges and continue working away at them, in time the ability of perseverance necessary for ultimate success begins to be created. However miniscule that ability might initially be, things become that much easier to handle. This ability to persevere buttresses your own resolve to persist, and as a result your efforts gradually become less belabored. This new ability, in turn, creates yet higher ability, ensuring, in other words, that your perseverance now lasts longer.

Letting the Workings of Nature Guide Us

If you are unable to withstand the challenges and quit halfway through, you return to the starting point. No matter how many times you repeat this process, you cannot escape from the difficulty that requires overcoming. In the end, you give up entirely, thinking the pursuit was hardly possible to begin with, and you lose hope. The unhappiness of many youths comes about in this way. Let's consider the example of the seeds of a tree.

Let us say that you bury a seed underground. It does not easily sprout. Yet, although it is invisible, the moment you bury it the seed begins to germinate. This unseen process embodies the workings of nature, while also corresponding to the basic operation of rationalism. You must not impatiently dig out the seed. (The same applies to the earliest stages of the development of human ability.)

Now it has begun to sprout. Along with joy over its birth, the seedling inspires happy anticipation for its growth. Anticipation gradually increases. (This is the same as when ability finally begins to reveal itself in a human being.) At the same time, the roots of the seedling are stretching themselves out underground.

These roots will become the force behind the growth of the tree. (They are analogous to the source of ability in humans.) The willpower of the roots—is it possible that this is the origin of the word for perseverance in Japanese, *konki*, the "will (or spirit) of the roots"?

Observe the form of the tree as it gradually becomes taller and sturdier. In proportion, its roots too become thicker and longer as they continue to reach outward. The "will of the roots" can thus be considered a treasure for those who persist to the end in their endeavors.

Neither Make Haste, Nor Dawdle

To act with resolve is to live with hope, or to keep in view a lofty mountain. There will be difficulties, but there will not be despair. Nobody can reach the summit in a single bound. And as long as one desires to make the climb, one must approach it step by step. Never make haste. This is a basic principle. One accomplishes nothing if one hurries and falls. Never dawdle either. This too is a basic principle. If one continues, regardless of what anyone else says, to move one foot before the other in silence, and without hurry or rest, one will never fail to reach the goal.

Next, throw yourself into your endeavor with unflagging perseverance and extreme patience—this level of commitment is absolutely necessary in developing what is called *kan*, or intuition. Permit me to share two actual examples of how intuition makes a task easier and thus proves to be a great source of strength when striving toward an accomplishment. I believe, for example, that had the Nobel Laureate Yukawa Hideki not cultivated his intuition, his meson theory of nuclear forces would never have materialized.

– 5 –
A Blind Child Sees

A Speck of Light for This Child in the Dark of Night

One morning, the oil painter Tanaka Sanekazu appeared with a letter of reference from a friend of mine, holding the hand of a charming little boy. The boy was blind.

"This is my son Teiichi—he's five. His eyes were afflicted when he was an infant, and because his life was at risk my wife and I had his eyes removed. As parents, we want to shine at least one light in our child's life to brighten the darkness. Music would be just the thing, we thought, so I am here to request violin instruction for him."

Tears came to my eyes when I looked at the young Teiichi, destined to grope his way through life, seated before me. But how was I to teach a little sightless child? I was wholly inexperienced when it came to his special needs. I therefore could not bring myself, on the spot, to accept him as a student.

"Please let me give it careful thought for one week," I answered. "If at that point I feel confident that I am up to the challenge, I will agree to teach him."

That night, after settling down in my study, I thought about the difficult question posed to me that day of how to teach violin to a sightless child. I was completely at a loss. From the outset, it was something I could never have figured out simply by mulling it over. After a while, however, an idea occurred to me.

"Why, of course! I need to place myself in the situation of the blind before thinking any further."

I rose and shut off the light.

The Eyes Are Not What See

When I sat and thought afresh in the dark, I could perceive neither up and down nor right and left.

"What is a child living in this pitch darkness to use as indicators for his conduct? In such a realm of nothingness . . . "

An invisible violin, and an invisible bow. To carry the bow in a straight line on a particular string without touching the other strings, guided by the minute difference in height amongst the four strings—this is the difficulty in violin playing. How was I to let the child understand this? I hesitantly made my way over to my violin case in the total darkness, and pulling out my violin and bow, I tried playing a few notes.

To my surprise, my playing was exactly the same whether it was light or dark. Long used to the violin, I experienced no inconvenience with my eyes closed. Even in the dark, I was able to perceive clearly the positions of my bow tip, strings, and bridge. They were clearly "visible" to me.

Until then, I had entertained no particular thought when I played with my eyes closed. But this was a true revelation. I realized that we are not dependent upon our physical eyes. We play music with the sensory power we call *kan*, or intuition.

When, after innumerable hours of training, an ability develops enough to be part of us, we begin to act in all areas by means of the workings of our life forces—a staggering power that unconsciously functions within us, or, stated differently, that we call intuition. For that very reason, I realized, I was able to play without impediment even though I had put myself in a world where I was unable to see either up and down or left and right. And so—

Opening Up His Mind's Eye

Yes, my task would be to help Teiichi "see" just as I was able to "see" the violin strings and the tip of the bow in the dark. He would not need visual sight for this, as long as I helped his mind's eye learn to see.

That was how I settled on my basic instructional principle for working with Teiichi. Now I only needed to think about a method for implementing it. The promised interval of one week passed, and Mr. Tanaka visited again with Teiichi. I told them, "I'd like to propose that we use our combined strengths and try our hardest to open up Teiichi's mind's eye." I also requested that Mr. and Mrs. Tanaka prepare themselves to make herculean efforts, and to persevere to the end.

This was how Teiichi's lessons started. I must note that the Tanakas carried out their task admirably, even taking into account that it was for their child's happiness. Their inexpressibly painstaking efforts were subsequently to come to fruition, producing the light they had longed for in Teiichi's heart.

For a Little Child Unable to Distinguish
Up and Down from Left and Right

Our very first activity involved training to make the bow visible to Teiichi.

"This is what a bow is like," I said, letting him hold one in his little hand. I wanted to acquaint him with it by letting him pass his fingers over it from the frog and screw to the tip. Then, I taught him how to hold the bow, and after explaining which way was the top of the bow and which was the bottom, I commanded him:

"Try moving your bow up and down."

His hand, however, moved diagonally.

"Right and left this time," I told him.

The movement was again diagonal. Teiichi lived in a space with no up and down or left and right. In supposedly moving something up and down or right and left, all that this little child had the capacity to do was to move it diagonally in the selfsame way.

"All right, then. Let's make this your homework for the coming week," I suggested. "I want you to be able to move the bow up and down, and also to the left and right."

Naturally, there was no telling whether this could be accomplished in one week. However, I intended this first assignment to serve as a means for Teiichi to have fun while either holding the bow or touching it, and thereby eventually being able to "see" it. Needless to say, this homework for Teiichi was the Tanakas' homework as well.

A week later, I was pleased to see they had devoted themselves to completing the homework. Although moving in an arc, Teiichi's right hand, with the bow held in it, not only demonstrated clear vertical directions but was also capable of making right and left motions.

To refine this—to teach the hand to move in a straight line—was our next task. As time continued, Teiichi's homework gradually increased in complexity. The following anecdote portrays the scene of one of our practice sessions.

The Little Mouth Says, "Yes, I See It"

"This time, let's play a game. We're going to 'catch' the tip of the bow with our left hand, all right? Now, hold the bow in your right hand . . . You can *see* the very tip-top end, yes?"

"Yes."

"Now, then, try to catch that tip with your left hand. Here's the tip of your bow. When you catch it, you mustn't grope for it. Grasp it in one motion. Do you think you can do it? Go ahead, now, and catch it."

Amused, Teiichi gave it a try. But his left hand wound up grabbing in unexpected directions. As he happily played over and over again without success, his parents gazed, as if in prayer, at their son's hand. Finally his left hand was able to grasp the tip.

"Marvelous! The next step is to catch the tip five times in a row without missing. Let's make this your homework for next time."

This was the start of a game that was extremely interesting to the sightless child. Nevertheless, to grasp the tip five times in a row was no mean achievement. Even if he succeeded four times, failing in the fifth attempt meant that he had to start over again. In the course of repeating this endeavor, however, Teiichi made steady progress.

"You can see the tip, right?"

Whenever I asked him, he invariably answered,

"Yes, I see it."

What does it really mean to "see"? As Teiichi's little mouth, belonging to a child with no knowledge of the world as seen through the eyes, answered thus in its innocence, his voice moved me to sudden tears from time to time.

Succeed in This, and You Will Be Able to See

Although Teiichi was coming to me for violin lessons, he was thus far training daily with only a bow. This was because the *kan* or "intuition" of knowing the tip through and through was of utmost necessity.

Teiichi's next assignment was to learn to poke his left hand with the bow tip. It was imperative that I help him become thoroughly capable of *seeing* the location of his tip. I myself was able, when playing in the dark, to feel clearly where my tip was, and where it was traveling in relation to my violin. I had to make the same happen for Teiichi.

The formation of intuition for the bow would mean that Teiichi could overcome the first and greatest barrier in learning to play the violin. I believed that, once he had accomplished that, he would be able to follow his intuition wherever it took him.

To meet his left hand with the tip of the bow—this was quite a challenge for a sightless young child. It seemed to have been an intriguing game for Teiichi, however; he and his parents tirelessly continued his home training, and he kept showing improvement at each lesson.

After three successful strikes of his left hand, the tip of his bow might make contact with nothing but air on the fourth try. His childlike voice would call out, "Oops, I missed!"

"Too bad!" I sympathized, then encouraged him to continue. "Let's start over again. See if this time you're able to strike it five times in a row."

Nothing other than training can develop intuition, but if one trains with perseverance, intuition is certain to develop. Soon, Teiichi came to be able to strike his hand five or even six times in succession.

His next assignment, then, was to practice hitting his left thumb with the tip of the bow. To strike that small a point—my thought was that once he was capable of doing this, it meant that he had truly come to *see* the tip.

After One Year's Grueling Struggle

The laborious nature of this particular assignment for the Tanaka family can be surmised from the first aside that Mr. Tanaka ever let out.

"This last homework was more difficult than usual. We had a tough time with it . . . "

That was at the end of the first week. But two weeks later, Teiichi was able to meet his thumb two or three times out of five.

"Let me try, too," I offered.

I was certain it would be effortless for me, being sighted. I carefully took aim, then tried to hit my left thumb with the bow. But the tip swerved in the air, failing to connect with my thumb. I tried again, and failed a second time.

When I finally succeeded, my heart ached. I had assigned a sightless child, only five years old, to do what even I, a sighted person accustomed to wielding the bow, was unable to do. Not only that, I had assigned him to practice it daily for two weeks—what a cruel experience I had put him through!

I have no idea what countless number of times Teiichi had to try before he was able to hit his left thumb two or three times out of five. His parents' and his own perseverance won at length, however. His intuition had developed beautifully.

Once the child was undoubtedly able to *see* the tip of the bow, we began working with the violin as well. There is no way to describe his efforts as anything but deeply moving, and often grueling. A year later, Teiichi was as able as ordinary children to play a variety of pieces. When my young students, including Arimatsu Yōko, Toyoda Kōji, Kobayashi Takeshi, and Kobayashi Kenji performed at the Hibiya Public Hall in Tokyo, the six-year-old Teiichi played a Seitz concerto. Observing the sightless child absorbed in performance, many in the hall were brought to tears.

– 6 –
Intuition, Too, Is Something We Create

An Encounter With Marquis Tokugawa Yoshichika

Let me now tell you a somewhat boastful story about intuition. My father, who owned the Suzuki Violin Factory, enrolled me in a commercial school with the intention of employing me in the future at the factory. During summer vacations, therefore, I always worked at the factory and in addition acquired a general knowledge of violin making. Upon graduation, I formally joined the factory staff, and kept myself happily busy as a member of the shipping section, where I was responsible for packing merchandise and keeping the account books. Barely more than two years later, however, I began to run a slight fever in the evenings, and was ordered by the doctor to convalesce.

Starting in late fall, therefore, I stayed for three months at an inn in the coastal city of Okitsu in Shizuoka prefecture. While there I became acquainted with a Mr. Yanagida and his family, who lodged at the same inn. They were there, the four of them—the couple and two small children—from Hokkaidō, and I, who was always fond of children, instantly bonded with them. Mr. Yanagida told me that he had been a classmate of the botanist Tokugawa Yoshichika when they attended the Peer's School.

Late the following spring, months after my return to Nagoya, I suddenly received a letter from Mr. Yanagida, in which he mentioned that Marquis Tokugawa and his group were about to embark on a one-month exploration and biology research tour of the Kuriles in August. Mr. Yanagida, furthermore, suggested that I join the expedition.

My father being agreeable to this invitation, I visited Tokyo to obtain permission to participate in the trip. In Tokyo, I would meet Marquis Tokugawa for the first time, an encounter that inexorably led my fate in an entirely new direction. As I state below, at the time I was also undergoing a great awakening to life through reading the work of Tolstoy.

In the 40-odd years since then, it is hard to say how much I have been given in my life, on the one hand, by the progressive thinking of Marquis Tokugawa, and on the other hand, by the outsize character of the philosopher who constantly lived in truth.

Encountering Professor Kōda Nobu

It was 1919. Our boat was the 1,300 metric ton Chīfū-maru that carried provisions to various fisheries in the northern Kuriles. The exploration team consisted of 13 people: Marquis Tokugawa, Mr. Yanagida, members of the Tokugawa Biological Research Center, and several guests, namely the pianist Kōda Nobu, Marquis Tokugawa's older sister Mrs. Matsudaira, her son, and I.

Professor Kōda was the younger sister of the novelist Kōda Rohan and of Navy Lieutenant Gunji Naritada. The lieutenant had, in the 1890s, spearheaded Japanese migration to the northernmost island of the Kuriles, Shumshu, with an aspiration for national land development. Professor Kōda participated in the trip out of a desire to visit the Kuriles and commemorate her brother's achievement as the first Japanese national to settle them.

Even in August it was cold in the northern Kuriles, its sea and sky of such an intense blue that I felt both powerfully drawn to the waters and transported by the sky. Seals, schools of whales filling the whaling bay of Shumshu, and a field of wildflowers glowing radiantly beneath the sun on the remote island— the landscape of the Kuriles was like nothing I had ever seen, and everything made a strong impression on me. There were also warm relationships aboard the ship, and while impressions from landscapes may fade when we become used to them, delightful and elevated interactions among humans remain in our hearts permanently.

I was inseparable at the time from my violin. There was a piano in the ship's salon, and I sometimes played my violin, which I had brought with me, to Professor Kōda's piano accompaniment. Looking back on my youthful obliviousness to her extreme generosity, my face perspires from embarrassment.

Our boat moved from island to island and finally arrived at Shumshu. We disembarked to walk along the shoreline of Kokutan point on the northern tip of the island, when we spotted, atop a steep cliff at a height more or less within a stone's throw, a cluster of rare, reddish-blue moss.

An Illicit Stone Hits Its Target

"There must be a way to get that moss somehow," said Professor Emoto of the Biological Research Center, as he covetously looked up. I borrowed a tiny shovel for collecting specimens from a member of the center, and despite my best instincts could not refrain from volunteering my assistance.

"You needn't climb up there, sir; I will get it for you from here."

In elementary school I had a facility for catching cicadas by knocking them off trees with pebbles. I had also been a pitcher at one point when I played baseball while in commercial school. In short, I had some confidence in my physical capabilities. However, when Professor Emoto took me up on my offer and I stood directly under the moss gripping the shovel, the plant seemed to be a great deal farther up than when I had seen it from the side. *Oh dear,* I thought, but there was no turning back. In front of the whole group, I took aim and threw the shovel.

"Well done!"

The shovel successfully shot into the moss. Against my anticipation that it would bounce back, however, it remained stuck, refusing to drop back down. I would completely lose face if I left it at that. Several years earlier, I had thrown a stone at a sparrow perched on a branch and unintentionally killed it. Since then, I had stopped throwing stones, but I now found myself grabbing a fist-size rock.

"Watch how I finish this off. If I give a little tap on the handle with this rock, the shovel will fall straight down."

Even though the group laughed in response to my foolish patter, I was secretly in agony. The rock that I thus desperately threw just happened to hit the handle of the shovel. Together with the moss, it fell to my feet. What a relief! Listening to everyone's applause, I pledged to myself that I would never do anything like that again.

Intuition Must Also Be Created

My childhood training in stone-throwing unexpectedly came to be of service in the hinterlands of the northern Kuriles. Intuition saved the day, with a decisiveness that I found astonishing.

Intuition, I realized, was the certainty with which a skill instantly worked on the basis of rational experience. Without training, intuition does not develop. People only *think* that intuition is inborn. If intuition unexpectedly reveals itself, however, it is because unconscious training has been amassed somewhere along the way.

To cultivate intuition for a skill—the only way to achieve this is to train in earnest. Certainly, the way intuition behaves differs between someone who has trained from early childhood and someone who has not.

Admittedly, what one person can do after 500 repetitions may require 5,000 repetitions for someone else to accomplish to a similar degree. Seeing the difference in the rate of acquisition between such people, others often discuss the presence or absence of innate intuition, skillfulness or clumsiness. However, they may err in their judgment unless they trace back to the days of each individual's birth, research both of their personal histories, and consider how their present forms of ability have evolved. This brings us back to the argument that what is important is to place children in a good environment from birth and let them train efficaciously; but one must not forget either that those who do not succeed after 500 times can yet develop a desired skill after 5,000 times.

If one tries, one will succeed. Intuition develops. I was not an innate "master stone-thrower." At present, I am painting watercolor pictures in my own self-styled fashion. This is exactly what the old saying calls "starting calligraphy at age 60." However, painting has brought delight not only to me, but to many people, including Americans, who enjoy my modest attempts while their purchases also provide funds to assist my Talent Education movement.

I would like to note here that I only need to listen to someone's tone to deduce the performer's character, the quality of the posture and the bow-hold, the positioning of the elbow . . . in short, everything. Every year from December through January or February, I receive a thousand and several hundred Talent

Education violin students' taped graduation performances. After listening to them, I send them back with recorded comments on their spirit, posture, and physical movements. People wonder how I can infer such things simply from one hearing. I have no doubt that I owe it to the intuitive abilities that have been nurtured by over 30 years of training.

4

Destiny
My Path in Life: I

Dr. Suzuki at work.

– 1 –
An Immovable Fact

A Life Expectancy of 10 More Days

This all happened in late 1945, around the time when I made the decision to move from Kiso-Fukushima to Matsumoto. I had recently established Talent Education at the Matsumoto Academy of Music, but my digestive organs, which had given me trouble from the time I was about 20, were in even worse condition than usual. To recuperate, I lived alone in a rented room at the Asama hot springs, beyond Matsumoto, and cooked my own meals.

Cooking for oneself is a bother and tends to result in poor health. Even now I will go without eating for an entire day in the absence of someone else to do the cooking. During those days in Asama, I used to make some soup, throw in a few pieces of rice cake, and eat once they were stewed. Later I would toss more rice cake into the leftover soup and eat the same soup again. In the course of repeating this one day after the next for my three daily meals, my health gradually deteriorated.

My younger sister rushed to my side from Kiso-Fukushima. According to the doctor, my problem was neither cancer nor a stomach ulcer, but rather intense gastric atony. The ailment was dulling my mental and physical perceptions, while at the same time leaving my now inactive stomach in excruciating pain.

Despite the bitter cold of icy Shinshū, I was crawling, unawares, out of the *kotatsu*—a low-built, heated table under a blanket—and making my way to a corner of the room, groaning and pressing my forehead to the wall. My sister was shocked to see that I no longer felt the cold. At least I still had the strength to crawl at that point; soon I could not even muster the strength to get out of bed.

That was when Koike Misako, a piano instructor at the Matsumoto Academy of Music, visited to inquire after my health. Alarmed by the state in which she found me, she rushed out and brought back a certain Dr. Uehara, a highly regarded physician of Chinese herbal medicine.

"He's extremely fragile," the doctor explained. "Another ten days and he would have been in critical condition. Fortunately, the patient merely has a weakened digestive tract, nothing else is wrong with him. He'll be fine in no time. Let's start his treatment right away."

Saved by a Skilled Physician

I had been following another doctor's orders to eat rice gruel and Western soups, but Dr. Uehara directed me instead to eat brown rice and pickled vegetables. I must admit I was surprised. But since I was at death's door, I put my faith in her and followed her drastic instructions.

What happened next is a marvel: the prescribed diet forced my stomach to return to an active state. A week later I was able to stand, and a month later I could walk slowly outdoors. Having been at the brink of death, I recovered my health and am still alive today, thanks to being noticed by Instructor Koike and introduced by her to the wonderful Dr. Uehara.

Years earlier, when I was convalescing in Okitsu, I had made the acquaintance of Marquis Tokugawa Yoshichika, whose friendship eventually led to a major career shift for me, from company employee to citizen of the world of music. This second period of rest in Asama gave me a chance to hone my skills at the arithmetic table. I worked not only on multiplication but also devised a way to master division, addition, and subtraction. I decided that if I recovered, I would apply those tables in my teaching as part of Talent Education.

The arithmetic tables, put to the test at Hongō Elementary School in Matsumoto over a dozen years ago, are now approved for classroom use by the Ministry of Education. They have been adopted by schools in a number of regions throughout Japan, including—or so I am told—Aichi prefecture, where I grew up. Some day in the distant future, the Talent Education approach based on "the original mother-tongue teaching method" is certain to change compulsory education. I have in mind an educational approach that produces not a single dropout, a pedagogy that is based on love, which is nothing other than the inherent desire of every human being to absorb the true, the good, and the beautiful. This pedagogy will be able to accomplish at least one thing over the nine-year course of compulsory education: it will help children become human beings who find pleasure in being kind to one another.

In any case, I am persuaded that I was able to outwit death, and to endure several related trials, by virtue of a single word: *un*, or "luck."

My Father Suzuki Masakichi and the Violin

I was born in Nagoya in 1898 (the 31st year of the Meiji period) into the home of Suzuki Masakichi, who happened to be the founder of the world's largest violin factory. The details surrounding my birth are something that I have no control over on "this side." In other words, given that those circumstances were determined on "that side," I must attribute my fortune, for good or for ill, to a greater force: absolute luck.

The Suzukis had, since my father's grandfather's generation, run a family business in Nagoya that produced *shamisen*, a traditional, three-stringed instrument. It was essentially a poor samurai household's sideline. My father, who was born in late 1859, in the last decade of the Tokugawa period, studied in the capital city of Edo (now Tokyo) in his youth, desiring to become a middle school English teacher; however, he continued to help with *shamisen* production whenever he was home in Nagoya. His dream of becoming an English teacher, especially during the Meiji era, attests to his highly progressive spirit. Before long, he began to develop an interest in Western musical instruments, in particular the violin.

The violin and the *shamisen*, it turns out, share a common ancestry. Five thousand years ago, during the florescence of Egyptian culture, an instrument called the "ravanastron" was interred in the pyramids of pharaohs.[1] Apparently, this ravanastron is the predecessor of the violin, *shamisen*, and some other stringed instruments.

Time passed, and in the sixteenth century, a Christian missionary played the viol, a forerunner of the violin, for Lord Oda Nobunaga. This inaugural performance of the viol in Japan took place in Ōtsu, along the shores of Lake Biwa. Unhappily, the melodic strains of this early violin disappeared from Japan after the Tokugawa shogunate's expulsion of Christianity; it would not be heard in Japan again until the Meiji era, when it came into widespread use.

Although I say violins were widespread, very few people actually owned a violin in the Nagoya of my father's youth. It so happened, however, that a certain instructor at a teachers' college owned one. "Please let me look at it just once, while you are asleep," my father implored him. When he finally managed to borrow the violin from this teacher, he spent the entire night drawing a plan of the instrument.

Unceasing Inquiry and Thorough Integrity

Finally, following one failure after another, Masakichi created his first violin in 1888. Following the establishment of a specialized factory and the upgrading of quality controls, my father's company reached a peak production rate of 400 violins and 4,000 bows daily. At a time when Markneukirchen, the

---

[1] The ravanastron, an instrument of Indian or Sri Lankan rather than Egyptian origin, is thought to have been in use from about 4,000 to 6,000 years ago.

largest village of violin makers in Germany, had only 200 workers, the Suzuki Violin Factory employed 1,100 people. My father had not particularly studied mechanics, but he continued to learn and make discoveries in new fields of interest for him, eventually acquiring 21 patents by the time of his death at age 86. From childhood, I was daily exposed to, and taught by, his passion for learning and his determination to increase his knowledge base. Indeed, I learned countless material and spiritual things from my father. In addition to learning to be diligent in my personal education, I learned from him, through the following example, that people must act with sincerity.

As a result of the worldwide depression of the '20s, even the immense Suzuki Violin factory was in the red. Still remaining today in Nagoya are three parallel city blocks designed by my father. Their names are Ume-machi, Uguisu-machi, and Hayashi-machi (Plum, Warbler, and Forest, respectively), with a fourth, Suzuki-machi, perpendicularly cutting through the three blocks at the center. Together, the block names represent Suzuki Baiorin, an indication of the considerable land and other assets he once possessed.[2] When managing the factory became difficult, however, he began to part with the land, piece by piece.

To Live Single-Mindedly, Free of Calculation

"I am responsible for everything," my father insisted. "Both the company and my private property exist thanks to the cooperation of the factory employees. I owe all of my productivity to everyone's combined strength. I'm going to reciprocate in kind by not firing a single worker until all my assets are gone."

Within several years, the situation had deteriorated to the point where we had to sell our house and the land on which the house stood. It was only at this juncture that my father reduced the number of employees—which he did only after helping everyone plan for alternative work—and moved the business to a small factory.

---

[2] The street names are a play on words. Plum can be pronounced "ume" or "bai," warbler can be pronounced "uguisu" or "ō," and forest can be pronounced "hayashi" or "rin." If you combine the latter pronunciations for the three names (without the diacritic for the long vowel), you have "bai-o-rin," or "violin."

To anyone who knew my father's former prosperity, the new factory would have looked rather humble. However, the move epitomized the sincerity of a man who did not view financial gain as his whole purpose in business. Drawing on the workers' own strengths and maintaining social trust, the Suzuki Violin Company survived the depression. And it quickly regained its momentum after World War II, thanks solely to my father's reputation of sincerity.

The value of being single-minded and free of calculation—this is what I unconsciously learned from my father. As a child, I was fond of fishing, and often went to the river district to catch crucian carp. After a day of pleasure, it was my rule to return the fish to the water before I left; it was my way of telling them, "Thank you for letting me have a good time."

Even when no immediate profit or other effect is visible in an undertaking, I try not to ask myself shrewd questions such as, "How will I benefit from this?" Instead, I believe in a brighter future for humankind, and thus I choose to lead a life that allows me not to have regrets when I face death, no matter when that might happen. Instead of immediately quitting anything new, I mean to proceed with my work patiently and single-mindedly. By doing so, I believe that I can achieve almost anything. I believe this attitude also to be the fruit of the legacy planted in my heart by my father.

– 2 –
Not Wishing for Heaven

Unfair Profit Is Always the Root of Trouble

One may be born into a rich family, or a poor one—but whichever the case, it is not by one's own choice. We can only call this luck. During my elementary school days, I played at the factory or listened in on the workers' entertaining stories; when I entered middle school, my father had me work with them during summer vacations.[3] That is how I learned the joy of work, a joy that I will cherish to the end of my life.

---

[3] Until 1947, "middle school" referred in Japan to grades 7 through 11 and "high school" referred to grades 12 through 14. Hence the author was 17 years old in his final year in "middle school." The middle school that the author attended was the city-run Nagoya Commercial Academy, which changed its name to Nagoya Commercial High School under the postwar school system. He attended this five-year academy between 1911 and 1916.

However, I grew up with little knowledge of the value of money. Perhaps it was because of this childhood ignorance that today I do not feel poor even when I am penniless. Years later, as an adult, I was once scolded for coming home by taxi during rough times, when a thorough search of the house yielded just over one yen to cover the flat-rate one-yen taxi charge. Even now, the room I use as both a lesson studio and a drawing room has stains from a leak in the ceiling, but I don't find it the least bit miserable; essentially I choose not to worry about it.

The post-WWI Germany of my study-abroad years suffered from dreadful inflation, not to mention rampant unprincipled behavior—both by Germans and non-Germans—that made the rise of Adolph Hitler, and the outbreak of the Second World War, seem nearly inevitable. As an example of some of the exploitation taking place at the time, I, a mere student, was approached with the following proposal: "A large five-story building is on sale. It's all yours at a bargain price of 10,000 yen. What do you think?" I declined, explaining that I had not come to Germany to make money. When I was beseeched by an elderly German woman, however, I did purchase a Guarneri violin for a mere 2,000 yen. Some people may envy my luck, but that transaction is not something of which I am at all proud. My personal thought on the matter is that, regardless of the era, whenever there has been unfair profit, people have unknowingly created the roots of future trouble.

You May Give, but Not Lend, Money

On one of those days in Berlin, I received a visit from a Japanese university professor who had helped me find my apartment.

"My wife and I have an urgent need to return to Japan, but we have no money on hand. I'm very sorry to have to ask you but . . . " he trailed off. In those days, first-class boat fares cost 2,000 yen per couple. With an additional 500 yen for spending money, they would easily be able to return home. I lent him that amount and requested that he return the money to my father in Nagoya.

Once the couple had departed happily for Japan, I wrote my father to request his understanding. His reply gave me a start:

> ... I sent you the money for you to use for your studies. How impudent of you to have then lent it to someone else—this is an outrage. From now on, you must never, ever lend or borrow money ... If you have that sort of money, I would advise you to learn to share it so you can experience hardship together with any of your acquaintances in need.

In my immaturity, I had thought that lending the professor the funds, for which I had no immediate need, would make no difference as long as they were returned to my father. My father's rebuke led me to resolve that I would never lend money to others again. That experience has since shaped my lifetime approach to financial matters.

The monetary philosophy I newly adopted at the time can be stated as follows: "Determine my monthly living expenses, save enough for a number of months according to my budget, and never divert that amount toward other purposes. Whatever remains beyond my basic living expenses, I will enjoy by spending it with my friends." Money easily leads to complications. But my father's instructions prohibited me from involvement in financial dealings, and although my approach may seem absurd, I do believe that I have thereby been able to avoid overextending myself, being deceived by con artists, or getting tangled up in uncomfortable relationships.

Feel Delight in the Presence of Another

Call it an attitude toward constant learning, or a lifetime approach to cultivating agreeable human relations, but my father also taught me about interacting socially with others. Travel on land in those days was primarily by train, and he told me, "When you happen to share facing seats with strangers on a far-going train, you should first feel delight for being with the two people across from you and the third person next to you, because the four of you were fated to be brought together."

"That being the case, be sure to greet them, however briefly, since that will likely start up a conversation. You should practice becoming a good listener. Since other people are pursuing a different life from yours, they are bound to be in possession of different knowledge from yours; the conversation is certain to result in your learning something beneficial about human society. Rather than talking yourself, try to draw out what others may have to say, and listen attentively. It will be a positive experience, since those other people will certainly enjoy talking about what they individually know."

I will later touch on the concept of greetings, which are central to human relationships. But my father's instruction to say "hello," when first encountering a stranger, has provided the foundation of my thinking and behavior, not only on the initiation of satisfying human relationships, but on humanity, love, harmony, opening up one's destiny, and running with opportunity.

I Do Not Wish for Heaven

I don't quite recollect when it happened, but at some point after I had moved to Matsumoto, a foreign priest I knew visited me one day at home.

"You must come to church more often and seek heaven," he said.

"Oh, no, Father," I answered, "I am no longer so arrogant as to wish for heaven."

Neither, of course, did I seek hell. The haiku by the Edo poet Issa, "Whether good is in store, or bad, I leave it up to the Beyond this yearend" had resonated with me, and I had learned more of such pure contemplativeness through Mozart's music.[4] I wish to live life to its fullest, always doing my very best, and if I am whisked off to hell I have no intention of complaining. I feel quite unruffled about it all, whatever the outcome.

I assist as much as possible with the work of the church, but I never ask for any blessings. I simply say "thank you" for the blessings I have thus far received. This also applies to Buddhist temples and Shinto shrines. If I trace this attitude back to its origins, it too was derived from my father's teachings.

For a while during my middle school days, I made it a nightly habit, along with three other boys in the neighborhood, to visit the tutelary god of our local shrine. We walked 500 meters or so through the dark streets, chatting about various topics on the way, then prayed to the god and headed back home. It was nothing more than that, but it was a genuinely pleasant daily activity.

---

[4] "Issa" (一茶, meaning "a single cup of tea") is the pen name of Kobayashi Nobuyuki (1763–1828), a representative haiku poet from Shinshū province (now Nagano prefecture) particularly known for his sympathy toward children and small animals. Haiku, a 17-syllable, one-line poem with a 5/7/5 rhythmic structure, is often translated into English in three lines, but here and elsewhere the translation reflects the nature of haiku as a one-line verse composed of two phrases. See chapter 7, section 1 for the use of Issa's haiku for memory training at Talent Education Preschool.

Stop Making Self-Serving Demands

One day my father asked me, "What do you say when you pray to the deity?"

I answered that I prayed for divine protection for our family. My father's response was, "You must stop making such self-serving demands. If you're at the shrine every day, a simple 'thank you' should be plenty. What more do you need than to thank the deity for that day's blessings?"

Since then, I only express my gratitude for what I have already received, no matter what shrine or temple I visit. This is because I realized that my father was teaching me that it is unacceptable to request something for myself in exchange for an insignificant monetary offering. He was suggesting that although human beings have a tendency to wish irresponsibly for all kinds of things, to pray with such self-centered motives is inappropriate. This all happened when I was around 17.

Age 17—a topic often featured in the social section of newspapers—is a crucial stage of life. In my personal history too, as I will discuss later, it was a stage worthy of special mention. This is because 17 is just about the age at which one starts using the *un* or "luck" received at birth as a basis for living self-reliantly, and for eventually opening up the possibilities of that luck.

Naturally, unexpected things like an accident or death may await us. No one knows what luck may be in store for any particular individual. But here is my thought: all of that is up to the convenience of "the other side." It doesn't help matters in the least to live in fear, worrying unnecessarily about every potential calamity. What is meant to happen will happen in any case. It is up to all of us on "this side" to live life to its fullest, and with constant hope.

– 3 –
My Encounter with Tolstoy

Bitter Chagrin at Having Deceived Myself

I believe that the foundation of my adult life came into being in the year that I turned 17. In a sense, I think I can say that I was born then. For this reason, although I have spoken to many people and have also written about what happened in that year before I graduated from commercial school, I am unable to convey my approach to life without referring to the events in question. I therefore will repeat myself at the risk of boring some readers.

One day I went into the office of my father's factory, where a thousand employees were at work. I caught sight of an English language typewriter, a novelty for me, and casually hit some keys. The head of the shipping section came by and cautioned me: "Master Shin'ichi, you don't want to strike the keys when it's not loaded with paper."

"I'm just pretend-typing." Caught on the spot, I fibbed.

"Oh, I see." Without ado, the section head left the room. He was no sooner out of my sight than I was seized by intense anger and regret. "What a coward!" I berated myself. "Why did you lie when you should have humbly apologized?"

Unable to bear it, I went home right away but I could not remain still. I went out to Hirokōji, Nagoya's main street. Perhaps wishing to forget the discomfort that obsessed me, I found myself entering a bookstore and arbitrarily began to pick up random books from the shelves. It was in the process of flipping through them that I encountered Tolstoy, wholly by chance—or, as I prefer to think of it, in accordance with my destiny.

"The Voice of One's Conscience Is the Voice of God"

The book in question was a small one, titled *The Diaries of Tolstoy*. Without forethought, I took it from the shelf and distractedly opened a page. Right then and there, my eyes alighted on the following sentence: "To deceive oneself is worse than to deceive another."

The stern words pierced my heart and shook me to the core. I barely managed to fight the trembling in my entire body. I bought the little book, ran home, and pored over it. Starting that day, I read and re-read the volume until it literally fell apart.

Tolstoy—what an admirable human being. This feeling of awe led me to avidly read his entire oeuvre. My self-formation thus proceeded with Tolstoy as my sustenance. *The Diaries of Tolstoy* never, under any circumstances, left my side. No matter where I went, I brought the volume with me. When I went to Germany to study several years later, at age 23, this book was in my chest pocket.

Tolstoy warned against self-deception and equated the voice of conscience with the voice of God. I was firmly convinced of the need to lead my life in accordance with this Tolstoyan philosophy.

Work, Reading, and Playing with Children

At the same time, I began to occupy myself less with schoolwork, studying only enough to avoid failing my examinations. Capturing my attention, instead, were books that explored how to lead a meaningful life; for example, Francis Bacon's *Essays* and other Western philosophical writings. Probably this interest, too, reflects how my mind worked under Tolstoy's influence.

Around the same time, I eagerly devoured the analects of the thirteenth-century Zen priest Dōgen. The *Shushōgi* (Meaning of Training and Verification) begins with the phrase, "To clarify life and to clarify death—this is a matter of the greatest importance for every Buddhist. If there is the Buddha in life and death, there is neither life nor death . . . " I began adopting a lifestyle in which I found the highest pleasure in reading such books, perspiring amidst the factory workers at my father's plant, and befriending and playing with the children in our neighborhood.

Later, my study and appreciation of Mozart's music led me away from the notion of Tolstoy's "conscience" toward an understanding of the workings of the "life force" itself as the source of every aspect of human existence, but I believe that the foundation of this conceptualization, too, was formed when I was around 17.

The existence of young children, which is nothing less than the joy of burgeoning life, came alive in my heart. Eastern philosophy, which pronounces us all to be endowed with life through the grace of nature, took root within me. This, I would say, was the process that informed my late teens.

Herein Was the Source of Talent Education

Back then, I often played with the neighborhood children. Whenever they spotted me coming home from elsewhere, they all came running down the street to me. Taking their hands in mine, I led them to the Suzuki home for hours of fun with them and my younger sister and brothers. I was simply fond of children. Presumably due to having been baptized by Tolstoy, I had come to discern such a quality of preciousness in four- and five-year-olds that at times I nearly felt like joining my palms in veneration.

Young children never deceive themselves.

They believe in others without the slightest hint of doubt.

They know only how to love, not how to hate.

They love justice, and zealously adhere to rules.

Seeking joy, they live vibrantly and cheerfully.

Unfamiliar with anxiety, they live in a constant state of blissful assurance.

Before long, I discovered that playtime with the neighborhood children was actually a useful learning opportunity for me. I longed to keep alive within me the innocent human posture I observed in those children. A revolution had swept through me. I feel that Talent Education, which was eventually to be my life's work, began then.

Many of the world's beautiful children turn out to be adults who harbor suspicion, distrust, injustice, hatred, strife, unhappiness, and darkness. Why is that? Is it simply impossible to help them retain their beautiful hearts as they matured into adulthood? This was the source of my belief that our educational strategies must certainly be flawed.

– 4 –
My Father's Smile

In the Blink of an Eye

The motto of the Nagoya City Commercial Academy from which I graduated was, "Character first, skills second." A framed calligraphy of this motto was on display in the auditorium. This principle is still deeply inscribed in my heart as a torchlight that illuminates my path in life. In fact, whether scholars or artists, businessmen or politicians, those who are superior in their chosen fields are accomplished first of all as human beings; to excel in their fields, they must first be admirable as human beings.

I served as class representative for four years, starting in my second year at this five-year school. As mentioned earlier, I did not apply myself to studying, so my grades were poor, but I respected and loved all my classmates. They loved me in turn, electing me class representative, perhaps because they saw virtue in my spirit to serve others.

At the time of our graduation exams, Student A cheated, and, noticing the deception, Student B loudly reported it to the teacher. Student A was removed from the aroused classroom. But the moment that the exam ended and students had wandered out into the hallways, Student C pounced on the hefty B. "What kind of a friend do you think you are?!" C bellowed as he slugged away at the tattler. Several other students joined in to beat B to a pulp. I was still in the classroom at the time, for it all happened in a flash.

Before long, word came for the class representative—me—to report to the teachers' room. Our homeroom teacher was waiting for me.

"It's inexcusable that everyone ganged up on one student. Were you aware of this?"

"Yes, sir, I was. I punched him, too."

"What?! Who exactly was involved? I want names."

"It was the entire class, sir."

"Do you find this to be acceptable behavior, young man?"

"I do not, sir. I believe that cheating is impermissible. But tattling on someone is a betrayal of friendship. We beat him up because we couldn't stand for this. Please punish us as you see fit."

A School-wide Strike

On returning to the classroom, I informed my classmates of the substance of my exchange with our teacher, then proposed an exceedingly wild course of action:

"I was motivated by a fierce sense of friendship. If everyone agrees, I'd like to ask that we stick to my story that all of us punished Student B. By extension, this very likely means we will collectively fail to graduate this year."

Even those students who had not participated in beating up Student B immediately raised their hands to indicate their agreement. Furthermore, everyone declared on the spot his willingness to repeat our fifth-year studies with each other again.

Soon, each member of the class was called up separately for questioning by our teacher. When we returned to school the following morning, 20 students' names were posted with their penalties. Starting with my name, 10 of us were to be suspended from school for an indefinite period; the other 10 were to be formally reprimanded. Our teacher had figured out by then that I had not joined in the beating of Student B, but the penalty was unavoidable because I was the class representative. However, the remaining 19 students were punished in proportion to how rowdy they usually were.

Naturally, many voices were raised in protest against the unfairly distributed penalties. While some students swore they would never submit to such inequitable treatment, one classmate went so far as to march into the teachers' room, demanding to know why he had received no punishment when in fact he had participated in beating up Student B. Criticism of the school's handling of the situation instantly spread across the entire campus, and on the following day not a single student showed up for class. Essentially, this could be characterized as a sympathy strike.

After a week of continued non-attendance by the entire student body, each of us received a summons to school. Gathering all 1,700 students in the auditorium, the schoolmaster Ichimura Yoshiki—who had put up the mounted calligraphy with the motto, "character first, skills second," and whom I held in particular esteem—addressed us through tears. In closing, he stated that he would assume, regarding the most recent events, that nothing had happened and that all graduation exams would take place anew.

The Smile Flits Across My Father's Face

Ours was a mediocre class that would under normal circumstances have produced two or three dropouts, but in this way, ironically, everyone graduated. This happened in 1915, already 50 long years ago.

On the very evening of the day of the beating incident, I had confessed everything to my father. Bowing respectfully, I informed him, "I will be failing the year instead of graduating," then asked, "May I have your permission to stay in school another year?" He smiled and simply replied, "It can't be helped now, can it?" The expression on his face was a truly venerable one.

When I was first called up to the teachers' room that day, I found myself able, just as I had been taught by Tolstoy and had learned from the neighborhood children, to speak honestly as my heart dictated, "without deceiving myself." I remember my surprise after I had spoken. And I think the solution to the problem was already contained in the answer I gave our teacher—my words acknowledged what was wrong as wrong, stated what I believed, and asked to be punished. They represented my genuine feelings, free of calculation. Guided by Tolstoy, the invaluable sentiment of friendship, or affection for others, was probably starting to take root in my heart.

I had affection for small insects as well. On my way home from school, through the grassy fields to the suburbs of Nagoya, I saw many ants, large and small, scurrying away at work. I recall trying my best not to step on them. Knowing that if I stepped on one ant, the vital force of that tiny creature would be eternally lost, I could not walk carelessly.

These were the kinds of days I spent in the years prior to reaching the prime of my youth. It was also around this time that, listening to my first phonograph records, I was stunned by Mischa Elman's "Ave Maria" and, at the same time, enchanted by the tone of the violin.

– 5 –
Up at Five

Winter Night Tales Heard at the Factory

Growing up in the violin factory, my brothers and I occasionally hit one another with the violins lying about when, for example, we were in the middle of a fight. To me the violin was nothing more than a kind of toy.

When I was in elementary school, even at night there were often 50 or 60 people laboring in the handiwork section of the factory, shaving violin necks and the outer surfaces of the top and back plates. Above each worker, a kerosene lamp hung from the ceiling to shed light on his work area. This was around the time of the Russo-Japanese War of 1904–05.

Nearly every night after dinner, I made my way over to the crew in the handiwork section. It was my pleasure to listen to the skilled storytellers among them. To this day, I can remember their names and their recounting of heroic episodes from traditional warrior tales about Iwami Jūtarō, Kimura Shigenari, and so on.[5] I fondly recall scenes of a man who told stories while working away under the lamplight, and a boy absorbed in listening to him.

On winter nights, when the story was reaching its climax, the narrator would comment, "I have to say, this is the right moment for rice cakes." Worried that the story might run off elsewhere, I would rush back to our house next door and grab precut rectangles of rice cake from a large barrel to take back to the factory. The narrator would roast them over the charcoal brazier next to him as he continued to shave wood, and resume telling his mesmerizing story . . .

Years later, following my admission into the commercial school, I worked at this same factory during my long summer vacations. In the process, I learned the basic steps involved in the manufacture of violins—from the mechanical operation of the machines, to the crafting of handmade parts, to

---

[5] Iwami Jūtarō and Kimura Shigenari fought for the losing side in the Winter and Summer Battles of Ōsaka (1614–15), in which the Tokugawa destroyed what remained of the Toyotomi clan. Iwami, a semi-legendary figure, is known for avenging his father's death and subjugating a wicked white-furred baboon and a giant snake. Kimura is particularly famous for leading his troops into a suicidal battle that ended his and many of his subordinates' lives.

the varnishing—and I came to know the joy of working assiduously. Still, I had not yet encountered the tonal beauty of the violin itself.

Listening to Elman for the First Time

I think it was sometime before I graduated from commercial school that a phonograph player found its way to our home. Instead of the electric motors we have today, it was equipped with a spring attached to a wind-up handle, and an amplifier called a bugle that functioned as a speaker. The bugle, shaped like a morning glory, was so large that a child's head could easily fit inside it.

The first recording I bought for this player was of Mischa Elman performing Schubert's "Ave Maria." I felt my very soul entranced by the sweet tone of his playing. A dream-like melody wrapped in velvety softness—I was shocked by the experience. For the violin to produce such exquisite tone, when I had never thought of it as anything more than a toy . . .

Elman's "Ave Maria" opened my mind's eye toward music. I do not know why I was so moved. But the ability to perceive its beauty had already flowered within me. It had been nurtured by Tolstoy and others whom I had read zealously. And this wonderment became the first step in tackling the question that came to preoccupy me: what is art?

I asked to take home a violin from the factory. From among the various pieces on the Elman record, I chose Haydn's "Minuet" because it seemed feasible for me to attempt, and I repeatedly listened to it in an effort to figure out how to play the violin. Without recourse to the printed music, I moved my bow across the strings day after day, trying to learn the Minuet. I pursued this in a wholly self-taught fashion such that the term "scraping" best describes my bowing style, but somehow or other I eventually managed to produce a violin-like sound.

Haydn's "Minuet" thus became my first specialty. Before long I was deriving substantial comfort from playing the violin, growing increasingly fond of it, and developing an unshakable attachment to music.

A 50-Year Habit of Rising at Five

As I wrote earlier, on graduating from commercial school I became a formal employee of the violin factory. The gates always opened at seven in the morning, but my family did not arrive for work until nine o'clock or so. This is because, from the perspective of the factory, my family members—specifically my father, my brothers, and I—were on the ownership side of things.

On my first day as a company employee, however, I deemed myself the same as the many workers. I felt that as long as I worked there, I could not differentiate myself as a member of the employer family, that such behavior was impermissible for me as a human being. If everyone else worked starting at seven, then . . . With this realization, I resolved never to be late for the seven o'clock start to the work day. This, too, may have been an attitude I absorbed from Tolstoy's teachings.

I rose at five every morning. I then woke my younger brothers and sister, telling them it was time for a walk, and shepherded them onto the train to Tsuruma Park.[6] At the park, the carp in the pond made ripples, waiting for the feed we had brought along. On returning home, I gulped down my breakfast and walked briskly to the factory, 17 minutes away on foot from the house we had moved to by then. Lining up with the other workers, I waited for the opening of the gate.

I should note that even now, I spontaneously wake up by five. The habit I formed during the approximately two years I worked at the factory, of always rising at five in the morning, has thus lasted for 50 years.

Once the workday came to an end at five in the evening, I would head back home. En route I always found little Tomi, Tatsu, and other children waiting for me. Practically swinging themselves from my hands and waist, the children walked with me in joyful anticipation of the fun they would have with me and my younger siblings. It was a fulfilling time for me: work was enjoyable, the violin was enjoyable, and the hours I spent chatting and playing games with the neighborhood children were enjoyable above all else.

---

6 Tsuruma Park, now more commonly called Tsurumai Park, was established in 1909 as the first public park in Nagoya.

Discontent Lies Entirely Within Oneself

The question might arise in some people's minds: was there nothing about which I was dissatisfied? I believe there was hardly anything I needed to complain about to the outside world. Discontent was always present within me, but my impulse was to complain solely to myself and then to improve myself accordingly. I had no desire, for example, to criticize my family members who went to work late as executives do. I simply felt that because the workers started work early in the morning, I myself had to do the same. This, for me, was the voice of conscience. I was trying to bring to fruition those words of Tolstoy, pronouncing the voice of conscience to be the voice of God, as part of my blood and flesh. To commit myself to whatever might be presented to me in a given moment—that meant to follow my conscience. At the same time, that act of committing myself gave me a sense of fulfillment, thereby infusing every aspect of my life with joy.

For that reason, I truly enjoyed the aforementioned journey to the northern Kuriles. And when Marquis Tokugawa Yoshichika, toward the end of the journey, suggested that I study music formally rather than work in the violin factory, and Professor Kōda encouraged me by seconding the idea, I did reply that I would think about it. But I hardly felt that it concerned my future; I knew that the reason my father had me working at the factory was to learn to assist in its management, and I could not expect to alter his view of my role there. Moreover, I enjoyed the work.

I had no fantasy of becoming a musician. To me, of greater import was the question, "What is art?" that had been occupying me as a result of Elman's awe-inspiring musicianship. Indeed, toying with the violin was, for me, more about gaining perspective on that question. However . . .

– 6 –
A Change in Direction

Lodging at the Marquis Tokugawa Estate

One autumn day in the same year as that summer trip to the northern Kuriles, Marquis Tokugawa came to Nagoya and visited our home. At one point he turned to my father and asked, "Why not let Shin'ichi study music? The pianist Kōda thinks he has promise."

My father had once conveyed his feelings about a musical career to me as follows: "No matter how fond you are of music, there's no need for you to do work that calls for you to bow obsequiously to large numbers of people. If you wish to listen to music, it ought to be satisfying enough to do a fine job in your own work, and to invite performers to the house to play for you."

Given his view, I thought he would hardly acquiesce to the marquis' suggestion. But he wound up replying to the marquis, "I'll go ahead then, and have him study music; I entrust him to you." As I mentioned earlier, this meant a completely unanticipated change of fate, triggered by none other than Marquis Tokugawa.

I began taking violin lessons the following spring, at the age of 21, with Professor Andō Kō, the younger sister of Kōda Nobu. I lived in a room in the Tokugawa family estate at Fujimi-chō in Azabu, Tokyo. I lodged with the Tokugawas because an initial plan for me to buy a house failed, a luckier outcome than any for which I could have dreamed. Brought even closer to the marquis, I had the good fortune to hear all kinds of stories while dining with him.

Additionally, there were almost daily visits to the Tokugawa residence by numerous teachers, friends, and scholars, including the physicist and essayist Terada Torahiko and the phoneticist Satta Kinji. Being placed among such impressive people further aided my personal development. Looking back on that time, I feel that Marquis Tokugawa was providing me in the most natural manner possible with a humanistic education.

Disappointing Graduation Performances at the Ueno Music School

My violin lessons with Professor Andō were once weekly. During one such lesson, she urged me to consider taking the following year's entrance examination for the Ueno Conservatory of Music, where I would be able to learn other subjects and not only the violin. I followed her advice and prepared for the exams.

Shortly before the exam day, on her recommendation I headed for Ueno to hear the conservatory's graduation recital. I went with high expectations but was extremely disappointed by the level of the student performances. The next day, I visited Professor Andō. "I attended the graduation recital yesterday," I told her. "With all due respect, I feel it would be a shame if studying at Ueno would take me no higher than the level of playing I heard at the recital. I've decided after all not to take the entrance exams. This may be a selfish request, but would you kindly allow me to continue taking lessons with you?"

The graduation recital had sounded terribly uncertain to my ears, trained as they had been through repeated listening to recordings of the world's superlative performers. I therefore thought I would be better off not being admitted into that school. Smiling, Professor Andō responded, "Either way is fine with me; just be sure to study hard." With no further discussion of the matter, we resumed my weekly lessons. That I did not enter the conservatory in Ueno eventually led the way to my studying abroad in Germany.

Yes, Work That to Your Advantage!

Besides my lessons with Professor Andō, I studied music theory with the composer Hirota Ryūtarō, and acoustics with the musicologist Tanabe Hisao, at their respective homes. About a year and a half after the commencement of my studies in Tokyo, however, Marquis Tokugawa decided to take a leisurely tour around the world.

"Why don't you come with me, Suzuki?" he proposed. "It'll take about a year, but it'll be fun." I had only recently taken up my study of the violin, however, and thinking that it would be fruitless for an inexperienced youth like myself to travel the world, I answered him accordingly. "In that case you must apply yourself to the violin," he said, and the topic ended there. Yet summer vacation came soon afterwards, and when I happened to mention the conversation to my father, his response was a complete surprise.

"Why, that *does* sound interesting . . ."

I looked up in astonishment, and he added, "I have nothing to worry about if you're going with the marquis. It'll be good for you to see the entire world once. I imagine that 15,000 yen ought to cover your expenses. Go with him, son."

Despite my father's encouragement, I still declined the offer. I could not bring myself to end my studies midway, before I had even learned all that much. In early September, back in Tokyo after my summer vacation, I conveyed my father's response to Marquis Tokugawa over dinner.

The marquis turned his impish eyes toward me, his chopsticks held aloft.

"That's marvelous, Shin'ichi—you'll have to work that to your advantage! Why not make off with the 15,000? You'll stop in Germany en route in our travels across the globe. And you'll study the violin there—this is so exciting! I'll trick your father into this when I'm in Nagoya next time."

Aboard the Hakone-maru, Guided by Tolstoy

My father easily took the bait. I'm told these were his words to the marquis: "I have nothing to worry about if my son will be in your company. I'm satisfied if he sees the world, and, if there is any money left over, for him to spend some time studying while abroad. It is indeed very kind of you to take him with you."

Although this may sound hackneyed, I still cannot refrain from thinking that a person's fate is unpredictable. Having been disheartened by the Ueno Conservatory of Music, I was aboard the Hakone-maru, a luxury boat headed for Marseilles, in the autumn of that very year. My father believed me to be leaving on a world tour, while I was departing with the sole intention of studying in Germany. It was October 27, 1920, or the ninth year of Taishō. I had turned 22.

As I noted previously, Germany at the time was experiencing dreadful inflation, and so I was able to spend almost nothing and yet live comfortably. Ten Japanese yen at first equaled 600 marks, but eventually was worth 10 billion, then 100 billion marks. Before I knew it, my plan to stay in Germany for a year had turned into an eight-year course of study, though naturally it was not all accomplished for that initial 15,000 yen.

This destiny was not something that I myself opened up. I felt like I was moving forward, led along by some other entity. At the time, that something ultimately turned out to be Marquis Tokugawa's boundless affection. Each day, I strove to be malleable, to have the heart of a young child. He approved of my efforts and enthusiastically supported them. After all is said and done, however, it was Tolstoy who constantly reminded me to be pliant and responsive in my engagement with my surroundings. I credit Tolstoy with opening up my fate; it was his heart that showed me the path to follow.

5 Embraced by Mozart
My Path in Life: II

At the Talent Education Institute.

– 1 –
The Soul of Art

Finding Karl Klingler on My Own

During a recent Christmas at home in Matsumoto, I received a small parcel from Germany. It was a gift from Professor Karl Klingler (1879–1971), who, at the ripe old age of nearly 80, was spending his days in Munich composing music and otherwise occupying himself. The gift was a copy of his unaccompanied violin sonata. As I reminisced about my teacher from 40 years ago, I was for a while oblivious of time, lost in memories of my days as a student in Berlin.

After I parted at Marseille with Marquis Tokugawa and his co-travelers who continued on their world tour, I went directly to Berlin, accompanied by a German engineer, Fügel, with whom I had become close friends on the Hakone-maru. Letting a room at a hotel, I wandered around the city for three months, taking in concerts almost every evening. After all I was there having declined Professor Andō's kind offer to introduce me to a teacher. I listened to all the performers without exclusion, ranging from rising talents to the well established. It was my attempt to find a performer who made me feel that *this* was the teacher for me.

After three months, however, I still had not come across such a person. I was starting to consider moving to Vienna, when I heard a performance by the Klingler Quartet. The location was the Sing-Akademie, and the person who took me there was Mrs. Kapel, a relative of Mr. Fügel.

Even now, if I strain my ears, the performance that night returns to me quite vividly. It was eloquent music of the soul. It enveloped my heart beautifully, and spoke to me with quiet intimacy. At the same time, the performance was characterized by disciplined, honed technique. Without even the benefit of an introduction, I wrote directly to Professor Klingler in English because I could not write in German: "Please accept me as your disciple."

After sending my letter, I was feeling disappointed because I heard from Japanese musicians in Germany that Klingler did not take students and that I hardly stood a chance of his making an exception for me. But then Professor Klingler wrote back, inviting me to stop by the following Wednesday.

I thus had the same experience as that undergone by the 19-year-old Toyoda Kōji, years later, when he visited Enescu by himself and became his student. Finding my way through the still unfamiliar city of Berlin, I met Professor Klingler and was prompted by him to play something. I chose a Rode violin concerto, but at one point I tripped myself up and had to replay a passage. I had halfway resigned myself to the thought that it was all over, but Professor Klingler generously asked me, "When can you come next?"

A Person of Inner Strength and True Courage

In this way, I started lessons with the teacher whom I had taken the liberty to choose for myself. I was his only private student. Professor Klingler was 40ish, with a strong build, and he made me feel right at home. He always emphasized the essence of music, above technique and all else. Before playing a Händel sonata for me, for example, he would ardently explain the composer's lofty religious feelings when he composed the piece. Professor Klingler gently led me by the hand, seeking the source of the artist and the art. I was fortunate to be able to taste the happiness of advancing under the guidance of his honorable character.

His friends, who invited me to the occasional recitals they held in their homes, were also wonderful. I cannot begin to describe how beneficial a learning opportunity those recitals provided.

I had returned to Japan by the time the Nazi movement was flourishing and Hitler had seized power. But I heard the following news, which vividly reminded me of the courage of my gentle teacher. At the front entrance of the Berlin Hochschule, where Professor Klingler taught, was a statue of Joseph Joachim, the leading violinist in late-nineteenth-century Germany. Joachim was Jewish, and Hitler ordered the statue removed. Alone among his colleagues, Klingler fearlessly protected the statue of Joachim, who in addition to being his teacher was a man of superlative artistic achievement. "We must never allow it to be demolished!" Still insisting so, he was finally driven away from the Hochschule.[1] This represents the magnificence of a human being who truly lived in art. It was from him, a man who possessed such greatness, that I received a formless yet enormous strength.

I Learned the Soul of Art

At lessons, I would play through my assignments at Professor Klingler's side, and he would stop me from time to time to offer guidance. A lesson in this format, going over everything once through, took at least two hours. Over the course of each lesson, Professor Klingler pointed to this, that, and yet another problem, with the result that I wound up with a large number of detailed instructions for my homework. He devised this multi-angled approach, I am sure, in order to remedy my many shortcomings, and he generously taught me without concern for the time it took.

Because I had a considerable streak of laziness, however, it was an effort for me even to superficially work through these many assignments. As I have

---

[1] Klingler also dissolved the highly regarded Klingler Quartet rather than dismiss the quartet's cellist, Ernst Silberstein, for being Jewish.

written, I eventually despaired over my performance ability. The root of that despair was based not in an absence of talent but in my ignorance about how to develop it: to repeat the same piece hundreds of times, trying to play it with ever greater refinement, beauty, and ease.

Professor Klingler, however, did impart to me the soul of art. My ultimate wish was not to become a performer, but truly to know what art is, and he helped me greatly in my pursuit of this goal. With respect to the violin, I studied concertos and sonatas with him during the first four years, and, during the second four years, chamber music. This was a natural development arising from both the fact that I gradually formed an interest in chamber music, and that he was a master in that field. All in all, I am able to say that in Berlin I did what I had set out to do.

– 2 –
Einstein, the Man

Dr. Einstein as My Guardian

Having found Professor Klingler, I decided to settle in Berlin and took a room at the home of a white-haired widow with three children and an elderly servant woman. Both the widow and the servant woman were hard of hearing, which meant that nobody complained no matter how loudly I practiced the violin!

In addition to this stroke of luck, I was fortunate enough to be warmly cared for at the home of Dr. Leonor Michaelis, a professor of medical science.[2] His family was exceedingly kind to me, in part because my family had invited the professor to our home in Nagoya when he visited Japan. At a certain point, when Dr. Michaelis accepted an invitation from the United States to be a departmental chair at Johns Hopkins University, he told me, "I won't be able to look after you anymore, but I'm going to ask a friend to take over for me."

---

[2] Dr. Michaelis (1875–1949) was a biochemist and physician. His early career was based in Berlin, but in 1922 he taught at Nagoya University; from 1926–29 he was a resident lecturer at Johns Hopkins University; and from 1929–40 he was based at the Rockefeller Institute of Medical Research. He is perhaps most famous for his 1913 co-formulation, with Maud Leonora Menten, of Michaelis-Menten kinetics, which explains enzyme reactions.

He then took me to the residence of Dr. Albert Einstein, the discoverer of the theory of relativity.

Wholly unexpectedly, I thus became acquainted with a brilliant, world-class scholar and the eminent circle of people with whom he associated, all of whom treated me with warm affection. This was the most incredibly fulfilling time of my life, but it was also more than that. It eventually provided the basic theory and confident purposefulness behind my promotion, years later, of the Talent Education movement for young children. My contact with Dr. Einstein's greatness as a human being began in the following manner.

All Human Beings Are the Same, Madam

One evening prior to Dr. Michaelis's departure for the United States, music-making followed a dinner at his home. Eventually the professor and his friends suggested that I, too, should play. Although I knew my ability to be inadequate to the occasion, I also knew that it would be ungracious to decline the invitation. I therefore simple-heartedly played my favorite piece, a concerto by Bruch, that I was then studying with Professor Klingler.

Later that evening, we were quietly conversing over tea. An older woman of about 70, who happened to sit directly in front of Professor Einstein, addressed him with the words, "I simply don't understand it." Elaborating on her puzzlement, she continued, "Suzuki grew up in Japan with a completely different sensibility than ours. And yet, I undeniably felt Bruch, the German in his performance. How could this possibly be?" Professor Einstein, who was young enough to be her son, paused a moment, then quietly answered her with a smile: "All human beings are the same, Madam."

I was powerfully struck by his words, and could barely hold back my tears.

The Astonishing Musical Ability of Two Professors

Professor Einstein often phoned me when there was a good concert. "I've bought tickets," he would say, "so let's go together."

The violinist Adolf Busch (1891–1952) was a close friend of his, and Einstein spoke very highly of his character and performance skills. For Busch's concert, too, Professor Einstein called me as usual to let me know when we should meet at the bus stop. I arrived at the stop, taking particular care not to mistake the time, but he was there first, waiting for me. He accorded even a mere stripling like me the same solicitude that he would have bestowed on any guest. Truly humbled by his gesture, I was left speechless.

Dr. Michaelis was an exceptional pianist, and he always enjoyed accompanying Mrs. Michaelis, a graduate of the Vienna Music Institute's vocal department. At a home concert one day, Mrs. Michaelis, in a whisper, asked her husband to lower the key by half a step because she had a slight cold. Answering, "Yes, of course," he effortlessly transposed the accompaniment as requested. Moreover, it was a difficult song by Brahms, and he played without any music. I was simply amazed.

Just as Dr. Albert Schweitzer in his youth had struggled with the question of whether to pursue a career in medicine or music, Dr. Michaelis was also torn between entering medical school upon completion of his undergraduate studies, or making a living through music.

As everyone knows, Professor Einstein was a fine violin player. No matter where he went, he was never without his violin. His signature piece, Bach's "Chaconne," was truly magnificent. Ah, the feathery light movements of his fingers and that beautiful, tender sound . . . My playing, in comparison, was clunky, for even though I willed myself to play lightly and with ease, in actuality I elicited nothing but resistance from the instrument, resistance that was reflected in the sound I produced.

Young Kaufmann's Impromptu Pieces

Dr. Michaelis, a physician, and Professor Einstein, a physicist, vividly demonstrated to me, without ever putting it in words, the many meanings that a study of music can offer to human beings. However, before writing about this, I would like to recount another unforgettable experience.

One night, following dinner at Professor Einstein's house, we enjoyed a home concert. I met on that occasion an 18-year-old youth by the name of Kaufmann who was studying composition at the Berlin Hochschule. Eighteen,

I should note, was about the age at which I began experimenting in my own fashion with playing the violin.

Professor Einstein introduced the young man to the audience with the words, "Tonight, we will listen to some impromptu compositions by Kaufmann. Let me give him this . . . " and plunked out on the piano a short melody that was to be the theme. The young man rose and said, "I'd like to start with composers from earlier periods. First let me try a fugue in the style of Bach."

I was shocked to the core. The piece that flowed from the theme that Professor Einstein gave him was performed with astounding precision and beauty that invoked not only Bach's harmonic structures but even conveyed his personality. When the fugue came to an end, someone requested Chopin.

"Very well, I will now play a nocturne in the style of Chopin."

The nocturne began on the same theme proposed by Professor Einstein. Ever so naturally, it turned into a zestfully performed Chopinesque work with a beautiful, plaintive melody that suggested a flowing river.

In this manner, Kaufmann continued forth with one lovely melody after another, eventually treating us to Brahms, Beethoven, Johann Strauss, and Gustav Mahler. This all would have been impossible had he not absorbed to an exceptionally sophisticated degree those many composers and their styles. Additionally, the performances, entirely devoid of hesitation, conveyed how confident and musical the youth was.

Humble, Warm, and Deeply Thoughtful

The young Kaufmann's amazing improvisational abilities—whether or not this talent could eventually lead to a talent for composing is beside the point—greatly impressed me. The realization that this sort of ability can flourish, if properly nurtured, was deeply etched in my mind. What a joyous thought!

Professor Einstein and his friends were all experts par excellence in their respective fields. But each of them loved art, and they were extremely modest and kind. I was, to use a Japanese expression, a mere student boarder and novice with no skills to speak of, but I never once had the experience of being treated lightly or contemptuously by them. Instead, I was always enveloped by warmth and pleasure. Even their casual gestures in initiating conversation with me were evidence of their touching efforts to ensure that I would not be bored.

Two people cannot attain harmony unless one or the other of them acts naturally in concert with the other. Between the two of them, the one who does the accommodating is loftier than the one who seeks to be accommodated, for without the former no agreement would ever be reached. I learned this philosophy of harmony from none other than Professor Einstein and the friends he gathered around himself.

"All human beings are the same, Madam," Professor Einstein had said. The force of his words compelled me to harbor a dream: "If Professor Einstein and his friends are human, then Japanese children are equally human. Given their equality, I wish to raise these children as human beings who similarly possess a refined sensibility, modesty, and profound love for humanity." Years later, the impact of those words was still fresh enough to move me to wage my all in pursuit of realizing this dream.

"Music, the Impetus behind My Discovery"

Everyone gathering together and performing for each other, regardless of their skill levels—if only I could nurture children to become people who are able to experience this kind of pleasure in their daily lives, and who possess this kind of high intellect and sensibility. This has been a fervent and long-held wish of mine. I am not engaged in Talent Education in order to produce musicians, nor do the children participate because they want to become musicians. But anyone who has cultivated her musical ability to a high degree of accomplishment will demonstrate equally outstanding ability in whatever other field she chooses to enter. This was the case with Professor Einstein.

Moreover, someone once told me about the unparalleled beauty of the Einsteinian equations. I imagine that that beauty is the very beauty of composition engendered by the pure musical talent that Einstein possessed. He was only 16 when he formulated his initial idea of the theory that would later bring about a fundamental transformation to physics as it was conceived until then; here are his own words about that moment:

"It was my intuition that led me to perceive this question regarding the photoelectric effect on moving bodies, and I have to credit music as the driving force behind that. My parents had me learn the violin from the time I was six. I owe my new discovery to intuition honed in the world of music."

I am in agreement with Professor Einstein on this point. When, in later years, I leaped with astonishment at the wonderful fact that all Japanese children speak Japanese, I believe that what was at work, there too, was *kan* (intuition) that I had developed through the pursuit of art.

Placed thus among a circle of people with high intellect, sensitivity, and good will, I was truly blessed during my eight years in Berlin. During that interval, I was ultimately nurtured by the many performances I attended by European musicians. These performances, although initially causing me to despair over my own inability as a performer, eventually brought me closer to answering the question that had been haunting me: what is art?

– 3 –
A Great Love

Losing Both My Hands, Seated among the Audience

Of the concerts I heard in Berlin, I have more memories than I can speak of. Every one of them is still alive within me, and the memory of each one seems to become yet more distilled as the years go by.

Among those memories are, for example, the Berlin Philharmonic's performance of an Alexander Glazunov piece, which he himself conducted, and the female violinist, Cecilia Hansen, who performed the solo part for that concerto. The great composer Richard Strauss's magnificent conducting style. A concert of Pietro Mascagni's, in which he conducted a chorus of a thousand. A performance by Ferruccio Busoni on the piano, filled with a tenderness and beauty evoking the fragrance of white lilies in a twilight garden. This same piano in the hall where the Berlin Philharmonic Orchestra concertized produced an altogether different, gentle sound when Busoni seated himself in front of the instrument, conjuring up for the audience a lonely Beethoven bathed in warmth. The Sunday concert series to which the dignified pianist Artur Schnabel devoted performances of the entire cycle of Beethoven sonatas. Wilhelm Furtwängler, whom I often heard, was active at the time not only as the regular conductor for the Berlin Philharmonic, but also at concerts sponsored by the Society of Contemporary Composers, which introduced contemporary music from throughout the world; he left an intense impression in me of contemporary sensibility with his rendition of Schönberg's grand tone poem, *Pelleas und Melisande*.

Even amidst such a wealth of music, what captured me most was a work by Mozart performed one evening by the Klingler Quartet at the Sing-Akademie. The program that night consisted entirely of Mozart. And when it came to the *Clarinet Quintet in A Major, K. 581*, I experienced a sensation entirely new to me: I lost my hands.

The Immortal Light That Captivated Me

I am uncertain as to when I started thinking this way, but I consider myself to have been nurtured by Mozart, and through him, to have come to know love, truth, goodness, and beauty that transcend all reasoning. I am also profoundly convinced that I have arrived at this day having received his testament, lived under his guidance, and engaged in a social movement through which I work, in his stead, to advance the happiness of all children on earth.

The catalyst for all of this was the clarinet quintet performed by the Klingler Quartet. That evening, I was gradually drawn to the depths of Mozart's soul, and before I knew it I was so immersed in the moment that I was oblivious to everything; indeed I had even forgotten my own existence. Of course I realized this only later.

The performance over, I tried to applaud. But I had no hands at my disposal. Numb from the shoulders down, my hands were immobile. Amidst the endless applause of the entire audience, I was in a state of shock. Even when I regained my hands and my senses were eventually restored, I continued to stare vacantly.

An out-sized, indescribably lofty joy and excitement had carried away my soul. I had been blessed with entry into the world of Mozart's noble soul—

and at the moving thought that I had for the first time been able to perceive, through sound, the beauty of a magnificently radiant human spirit, I felt as if the very blood coursing through my veins was on fire. That was an infinitely lofty, eternal moment in which humanity transcended humanity.

That night I was unable to sleep a wink. Mozart, the human mortal, had set my heart aglow with eternal light.

Sorrow and Resignation Enveloped in Love's Joy

That was all in Berlin when I was 24 years of age. Ever since that day, I have received a massive and absolute power from Mozart. I am, in essence, an eternal child embraced by Mozart. What I perceived with wonderment in Mozart's music was his superhuman warmth. Transcending human knowledge and reasoning, it was a majestic and true affection that could only be felt by the soul.

Within the folds of this affection lurked profound human sorrow. It was an amorphous yet searing pathos that reflects the transience and loneliness of this life into which we are born, on this earth, and from which we eventually pass away. Mozart expressed this pathos with profound love, not only in minor keys but indeed in major keys as well. Life and death are workings of Nature over which humans have no say. As an expression of that inevitability, Mozart coupled that pathos with a deep sense of resignation.

Although in a major key, the clarinet quintet that night was suffused with this sort of wrenching pathos. Let's take a look now at the opening few measures of the second movement.

I should note, however, that it is impossible to view our pathos-infused, irresolvable human lives simply in terms of sad resignation. This is where Mozart's enormous capacity for love comes into play. Mozart warmly affirms human life, and all that it encompasses, with that great love of his. There is thus a transcendence of pessimism, and a reorientation toward affectionately embracing life as it is—and thereby experiencing the fact of being alive.

I listen to Mozart. In return, he embraces me with an affection that might be translated into the following words: "You, too, are a human being. You, too, are someone who, along with the great joy of being alive, harbors eternal sorrow. Humans are that way, all alike . . . "

Even Knowing That the Bell Tolls for Me . . .

That said, however, Mozart's love for human beings is not something that religiously casts light on the other world and thereby brings joy. "I don't object to sorrow in and of itself. Human life is sorrowful, after all. But, with love, life can also be a thing of pleasure and beauty. Can we not face the heartbreak in life by comforting one another?"

This is what Mozart tells me, and I wholeheartedly endorse his way of thinking. Later when I began studying the haiku poet Issa, Mozart's philosophy came across to me even more clearly. The following verses by Issa, for example, exactly replicate what Mozart conveys to me:

Whether good is in store, or bad, I leave it up to the Beyond this yearend.

That gong tolls for me, I know; and yet I take pleasure in cooling off this summer's eve.

The all-embracing heart of Buddhism is found, I think, in Issa's expression, "leave it up to the Beyond." His view of life is *not* one that says, "As long as there is no light in the next world, it doesn't matter whether I work or don't work in this one." Instead, it says that no human being knows about the next world. It says that even though this world is filled with sadness, love brings us much delight.

A cheerful, good-natured, and entertaining person—that may be the appearance on the surface. But anyone who lives while fully shouldering one's own grave would, like Mozart, answer as follows when asked what, indeed, life is about. Knowing that his existence is so small as to be imperceptible when viewed from outer space, such a person would nevertheless respond, "To live amidst everyone's love. A life that finds its meaning in this alone is the sole path to a truly worthwhile life as a human being."

This is what I believe.

Embraced in Great Love

The fact that I was born, and that I will eventually die, is the province of Nature. The moments in which we are born or die are never the responsibility of individual humans. Each of us bears no more than the responsibility to live. This is how I view the human condition.

Regarding my own life, I wish always to live in love and joy. No one starts out life seeking hatred and sorrow. And, I have found, it is none other than children who embody the very form of life that strives to live purely in love and joy. That is why I cannot help but embrace them.

Furthermore, I also embrace adults. What stirs this feeling is the compassion in my heart that tells me, "This person will likewise die." Mozart's embrace of me stemmed from the same impulse: "You, too, will die."

In his embrace I hear his voice, and I feel his great love with my entire body. Humans loving and comforting one another—therein is life. So has Mozart taught me; and so believing, here am I.

"You are equipped to make a difference, however slight, to help all children develop as better human beings and with greater happiness. Dedicate yourself to working for that purpose." With these words, Mozart gave me my life's work. I am convinced of this. I have, therefore, no desire for anything else. What everyone truly wishes for, without exception, is human love and happiness.

Therein Lay the Secret of Art

Love can be obtained only by means of love. In addition, our lives attain meaning only by means of love that involve the giving of love to others, for example, or offering solace to one another. Years ago I had discovered art and begun to seek, in music, the answer to what art is, and at long last art had given me work and a reason to live.

At one time, for me, art was at an immeasurable height a great distance away. Moreover, it existed in reality and with certainty. I sought out its secrets in the belief that anyone aspiring to art must travel a long way toward that object of envy and adoration. But during my eight years in Germany, what I finally awoke to was something wholly different from what I had expected.

The substance of art did not lie, after all, at such a height or distance. It was, rather, in a most ordinary place: within my own self. The development of my own sensibility, the way of being of my heart as well as its inner workings, and the happenings of everyday life—all of that constituted my own personal art, and it had no other choice than to be so. I realized that even the act of greeting someone was, as a form of self-expression, art. If a musician desires to produce outstanding art, he refines himself and gives expression to his more accomplished self. It is in this that his superior form emerges. If that same musician writes with brush and ink he likewise expresses this refinement in his calligraphy. Art, then, is not to be found in an isolated place. Works of art encompass in their entirety an artist's personality, sensibility, and ability.

As I mentioned earlier, on the one hand I listened endlessly to outstanding compositions and performances and placed myself in Mozart's embrace, while on the other I came into contact, through Professor Einstein and his circle, with high intellect, sensitivity, and humility saturated with human love. These two processes led me to my realization, allowing me to end my long quest. The question of what art is had already been resolved. All that remained was simply for me to work on my own. For me to refine myself anew, to orient myself toward greater heights—this would suffice.

Now, then, why indeed does music move people? This is a matter I will discuss later.

6 If You Think So, Then Act Accordingly

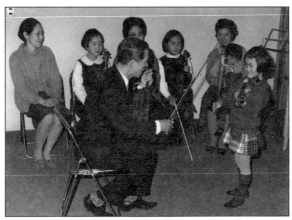

Teaching at the Talent Education Institute.

– 1 –
What Is the Use of Merely Knowing?

Sound Breathes Life—Without Form It Lives

One morning in 1953, I received a phone call from a newspaper company informing me of the death of Jacques Thibaud (1880–1953). The airplane carrying him had crashed in the Alps. I was asked to comment on the news, but such was my shock that I could scarcely respond. I stood motionless with the phone in my hand; it was the kind of shock one feels when notified of the loss of an immeasurably close, dear friend.

After the fierce shock subsided, I reflected on my sorrow with quiet tears. I had never met Thibaud. But before I even realized it, he had come to live within me. I loved and admired his violin playing, and from listening to his performances on record albums for over 20 years, I had sensed his character and studied his methods of musical expression and violin technique. Through music . . . through tone, Thibaud had, at some point unbeknownst to me, begun to live within me, and I was soon cultivating an unforgettable love and respect for him. Music . . . tone. What miraculous power it has!

It was on this occasion of Thibaud's passing that I awoke to a fact: humans do not live through wisdom; they live within the magnificent workings of life.

> "Sound breathes life—
>   without form it lives."

That moment of awakening was when these words became my motto. Fifty years ago, I had encountered Tolstoy's counsel: "The voice of conscience is the voice of God." To live with conscience had since been my inviolable creed, but from that moment forward "conscience" was replaced for me by "life."

Music—The Words of Life

In life, we submit to that which our lives seek, but what is this thing called life? The lives that we endeavor to live always face toward joy. If we allow wisdom to lead us, the results obtained are unnatural. If we adopt the innocent heart of a child, our lives—based on a foundation of love—will try to move toward the true, the good, and the beautiful. I believe that the Buddha's pronouncement, "Humans possess an intrinsic nature," expresses the same idea. I feel likewise about Mozart's heart, which has taught me that spontaneous love and joy transcend human sorrow. It was Thibaud who made me realize that this function of life was precisely what I most cherished.

At the same time that humankind created the culture of the oral and written word, it also created the superlative culture we call music. Music is a language of life that transcends the oral and written word, a living art that should also be acknowledged for its mysteriousness, and therein lies its capacity to enthrall. Bach, Mozart, Beethoven . . . all of these composers are vividly alive within their music, powerfully speaking to our life forces, purifying us, elevating us, and offering us supreme joy and emotional depth.

He is as young as a boy and wise as an old man—never old-fashioned, never modern, carried to the grave and always alive. His smile, which was so human, still shines on us transfigured . . . [1]

This is a passage from the pianist Ferruccio Busoni (1866-1924) extolling Mozart for expressing in sound a grand, formless being composed of his character and philosophy, as well as of his sorrow, love, and exquisite heart.

Talent Education Is Education Directed Toward Life

Nature imbues every creature with life. The workings of that life, or the force with which it endeavors to live, is far beyond human wisdom. Each and every person who becomes aware of this is compelled to esteem and value children, adults, and even himself more highly.

We are profoundly moved by the performances of Maestro Pablo Casals. In turn, the performances of children have the capacity to make that very same maestro cry and to move large numbers of people to tears. These all constitute beautiful symphonies of pure human life. The hearts, senses, wisdom, and conduct of humans, not to mention the functioning of their internal organs and nerves—each of these constitutes no more than a portion of the vigor with which we strive to live. Regardless of what it is that human wisdom gropes for or discovers, we must not forget to understand human beings as a unitary force—that is to say, as all-inclusive entities that revolve around the workings of life.

Accordingly, my Talent Education had to be education directed toward life, or stated differently, a pedagogy for life forces endeavoring to live.

Not to Teach but Foster

Why is it that every Japanese child develops with ease the superior ability to speak Japanese? That is where the secret of fostering human ability lies. When one does one's utmost to teach and to motivate children, yet somehow the results are less than fruitful, then surely the approach used must be

---

[1] From "Mozart: Aphorisms," written in 1906 to celebrate the 150th anniversary of Mozart's birth and currently published as part of a collection. Ferruccio Busoni, *The Essence of Music and Other Papers*, translated by Rosamond Ley, Philosophical Library, 1957.

misdirected somehow. This feeling of mine derives from the experiences I have personally undergone, and the experimentation I have undertaken, in the last 30 years.

Educators everywhere have become overly absorbed with the idea that they are *teaching*—they have forgotten the reality that a child's life *develops* of its own accord. Moreover, such teachers have failed to inquire deeply into the process by which ability develops. In other words, they have made the mistake of concentrating only on the *kyō* (教, teaching) part of *kyōiku* (教育, education), forgetting about the *iku* (育, fostering) aspect, even though the latter is the very aim of education.

At the level of elementary education, too, teachers are guilty of educating in ways that neglect to *foster* their students. Instead, they educate so as to *teach*, after which they inflict test after test on their pupils, who are then evaluated solely on the basis of their test results: this child is outstanding, this child is middling, and this child was born slow-witted.

Tests, by nature, should not exist to rank students. Rather, I believe they should be conceived as surveys to ascertain the degree to which students have understood a given body of material, and to discover if any of them did not understand something. I submit that the function of any survey chart based on student answers should be to identify which questions might be throwing off children who are confused or unable to execute particular tasks.

Depending upon how you view them, children's report cards are teachers' report cards as well. In schools today, however, they have become nothing more than children's report cards.

What Is Accomplished Simply in Knowing What One Ought to Do?

In theory, parents do not send a child to elementary school in order to have the child's *innate* qualities be evaluated through tests. Nonetheless, in actuality, these days it has come to seem as if human assessment, or the assessment of children through repeated tests, has become the job of the school, with the result being that everyone is obsessed with rankings. I find this to be unacceptable.

I would like to see schools help each child, during her nine years of compulsory education, to cultivate and solidify her abilities, even if it should so happen that these are confined to a single subject or skill. Nine years should be adequate for fostering in every child, at minimum, the splendor of having acquired at least one notable ability.

This ability does not even have to be in an academic subject. If, for example, education designed to foster a mindset and behavior based on "kindness to others" was carried out in everyday life at school, amidst friends, and at home, what a pleasant society Japan could create. However, the educational system today merely teaches children that they should "be kind to others." It therefore produces intellectuals who full well know that they should "be kind to others," but who are, in reality, fostered to become nothing more than unfortunate egoists. The current state of society is borne of this sort of education.

I hope that we are able, one way or another, through recognizing life as the source of children's development, to shift from education that teaches to education that fosters. This is why I have thrown my entire being into Talent Education. Stated differently, children have the capacity to develop in any way whatsoever, depending upon how they are fostered. May every child born on this earth develop into a decent and happy person, a human being with desirable abilities. I live always with this prayer, and stake my life on realizing it. I believe, moreover, that all children are born with the potential to respond to and to fulfill this prayer.

– 2 –
If You Think So, Then Act Accordingly

That's What You Thought, Is It?

This was during that miserable period following the conclusion of World War II. Winters in Matsumoto are severe, with temperatures at times dropping to -12 or -13°C (9 or 10°F). On one of those days, my younger sister Hina returned from an errand and announced, "I'm home!" Brushing off the snow on her coat, she said, "I just saw a wounded veteran standing out on the bridge in the dreadful cold, bowing his head to ask for donations. He was shivering in the heavy wind and snow, but it seemed like no one stopped to put money in the official donation box by his feet . . . I thought it would have been nice to invite him into a warm room so he could sit at a *kotatsu* (a table covered with a blanket and heated from underneath) and have some hot tea."

I immediately responded, "Hina, so that's what you thought, is it?"

Instantly agreeing and saying, "Oh, you're right," my sister ran back out to the street. I awaited her return by warming the room, raking the coals under the *kotatsu*, and setting out some sweets that we had received as a gift. About 30 minutes later, Hina returned with a man in a white robe that identified him as a wounded soldier.

"The lady here kindly insisted, so . . . " the man said in lieu of a greeting.

"Welcome!" I responded. "Please come in."

Kōji, Hina and I welcomed him to the *kotatsu* and chatted with him about this and that. After a while, he straightened his posture to address me: "May I ask what makes you treat me with such kindness?" "It's only that my sister wished to do this," I replied. "And so, without further ado, we have taken the liberty of inviting you in." "I ask because this is the first time . . . " he explained, then observed, "It was such a cold and awful day today."

A Need for the Ability to Put Thoughts into Practice

The veteran then spent two or three hours telling us stories from the battlefield and about his travels around the country to collect donations. Having thoroughly warmed up, he rose and informed us that he was headed for Nagano city. At the doorway, he firmly declined the donation we tried to offer him, protesting that he could not accept any favors beyond what we had already provided. I nevertheless sent him off with something for his donation box. "This is compensation for keeping you away from work for half a day," I told him. "Besides," I joked, "that box doesn't belong to you personally. So you probably have no right to decline."

Later my sister said, "I've learned a good lesson, thanks to you." More to the point, this was training for us all in the principle of, "If the thought occurs to us, let's act on it."

All of us experience on a daily basis any number of moments when we think it would be nice to do this or that. Everyone has the ability to think that doing something would be good or that doing something is necessary. But most of us stop at the thinking stage; very few of us carry out the thought. Directly after the war, I made a resolution when I realized that I myself was one of those people who merely thought without converting my thoughts into action.

"Mere thoughts do not constitute ability, since the result of thinking without taking action is the same as not having had a thought in the first place. Only when a thought is transferred to action is ability indicated. I need, therefore, to acquire the ability to follow up my thoughts with concrete action."

What, then, is the reason why so many people think, but fail to act—that is, why do they have no ability to put their thoughts into practice?

If All You Do Is Think, Opportunity May Slip Away

Since childhood, you may have been ordered or forced to do things by parents and other authority figures. Feeling rebellious, you may have developed an attitude of reluctantly obeying or deliberately disobeying such people, perhaps even to the point that this outlook has blossomed into an acquired ability.

When such an ability is operating without your knowledge, you cannot immediately switch to acting on your thoughts. The reason may well be that you have unconsciously perfected the habit of being someone who is unable to act spontaneously and naturally, even if you think of something you wish to do. But this is a tremendous loss in your path through life.

"Oh, I should have done it then," you may think, or, "It was an excellent opportunity, but I was too slow to grasp that precious chance." Lost opportunities may accumulate one after another, due to a person's lack of ability to put thoughts into instant action, until his entire life ends without luck ever turning his way. Always, he ends up with regrets. Chance, I should note, exists for everyone. Even when a chance is on hand, however, we may lack the capacity to take action. Taking no action means, then, that we have abandoned opportunity of our own accord.

If you must write a letter, or respond to someone else's letter, then write it immediately. You may think you will do so later, despite the fact that you are not in any way occupied at the moment. But one should promptly take care of even such a small matter, rather than dismiss it as trivial. The ability to do so is, in fact, very important. People who are able to perform many tasks quickly have the capacity to handle, one by one, and on the spot, whatever is necessary to address the concrete needs presented to them. Anyone who thinks he will complete a chore next time will be unable to do so, for when that "next time" arrives, another chore will be waiting for him.

As a corollary, then, those people who fail to do anything and end up with no particular results in response to an opportunity are those who continually postpone the things they ought to undertake. And this despite the fact that time can never be stretched. Yet, I have noticed that most people tend to fall into this category.

Everything Depends Upon Whether or Not You Act Promptly

Acquiring the ability to take action—I believe this to be the most important life skill for all people. Indeed, I would suggest that success or failure in life hinges on this alone. What to do, then?

In order to acquire the habit of acting on your thoughts—something that is much easier said than done—I recommend that you practice doing so today, starting at this moment. If you do so, I assure you that you will inevitably acquire the habit. Once acquired, it will serve as an invaluable ability. To know, but not to act—this is a flaw often seen among those who regard themselves as intellectuals. I may be repeating myself, but knowledge is merely knowledge, not ability. Only when knowledge has been truly internalized can it be said to be ability.

Many people know a great deal about baseball and like to comment on the games they see. However, such knowledgeable onlookers do not possess the intuitive ability, judgment, athletic skill, and rationality of those who have trained hard on the field and have become outstanding players.

To be frank, society is not in need of people who think about or ponder over the best course of action on such and such occasion. Rather, it seeks the aforementioned kinds of abilities that belong to superior baseball players. Using even the single example of baseball, we can recognize that training until particular habits become physically internalized in the body produces an ability that we can then apply in multiple areas within society.

– 3 –
Creating New Ability

Mere Self-Reflection Eventually Leads to Abandonment of Self-Reflection

I propose that action is inseparably related to that crucial activity known as self-reflection. A person with superior judgment has superior ability. Self-reflection, too, is a kind of ability to judge. Naturally, therefore, superior individuals are those with an outstanding ability for self-reflection.

Inadequate self-reflection during a period of personal development means that a person may inadvertently close off paths leading to self-enhancement. In other words, "Fortune shines on those who often engage in self-reflection." Yet at the same time, one can also say, "Unfortunate indeed are those who often engage in self-reflection." In fact, more people fit the latter category. Why? Because it consists only of empty self-reflection unaccompanied by self-rectification—there is only regret after regret.

Immersion in indulgent self-reflection makes self-reflection meaningless, and eventually leads to its abandonment. Reflecting upon oneself without changing oneself is equivalent to not putting one's thoughts into practice. Admittedly, self-rectification is extremely difficult. Unless we develop this ability, however, the light that illuminates our footsteps—the self-reflection that serves as our most valuable guide in life—will be extinguished.

How should we put self-reflection to good use—in other words, how should we handle self-rectification? Through music, I think of self-rectification in the following manner. Or, rather than what I think, let me recount some facts related to this matter. I have gained insight into the notion of rectification through my experience of instructing children whose intonation was problematic—that is to say, children who grew up tone deaf—in order to help them develop proper aural skills.

Rectification Is Impossible

In the case of tone deafness, many children produce overly high-pitched semi-tones; for example, with the note *fa* in the first four notes of the major scale, *do, re, mi, fa*. These children have already been nurtured to hear and produce a slightly high-pitched *fa*.

I have come to realize that nothing can be done about this past that has already been nurtured. In other words, this out-of-tune pitch cannot be rectified. It is literally impossible to correct the *fa* of a person who has mastered it at a slightly higher pitch. Then, what can be done to address tone deafness?

What I discovered was that although I could not teach tone deaf children to adjust their overly high-pitched *fa*, I could help them learn how to produce anew the correct pitch of *fa*. I decided that with a child who has become tone deaf from hearing the wrong *fa* 5,000 times, I would have her listen to the correct *fa* 6,000 times, then 7,000 times. At first nothing changed, but as she heard the correct *fa* 3,000 times, 4,000, 5,000, and 6,000 accumulated times, her ability to reproduce the correct *fa*, which she absorbed from hearing it 6,000 times, began to overpower her ability to produce the wrong pitch she had learned from hearing it 5,000 times. In short, the newly cultivated, correct function had taken root.

If you have made it this far, you are bound to succeed. Just as left-handed people favor their left hands, humans tend to use the better of their abilities. Because the correct *fa* became easier for her, this child came to rely solely on it. Her tone deafness, in other words, had been fixed. The successful completion of this process takes a six-year-old child six or seven months. This, then, is the method I discovered for replacing erroneous ability with proper ability. As I noted above, this involves the new development of correct ability, rather than the rectification of what is already there.

Not Rectification but Creation of New Ability

Experimentally speaking, let us place a child who grew up speaking Osaka dialect in a Tokyo-dialect environment far away from his home. If we catch up with the child 10 years later, when he is 16 years of age, he will have perfectly mastered the Tokyo dialect. The same logic applies here as with curing tone deafness. The child did not rectify his Osaka dialect so that it became Tokyo dialect, but instead fostered a new ability to speak Tokyo dialect. At a certain point, that ability became more powerful than his ability to speak Osaka dialect.

Now let's return to the notion of taking action. Based on the fact that self-reflection poses considerable difficulties, I have discussed the case studies above to suggest how to cultivate a new ability instead of rectifying an old one. But it is clear from the discussion that in order to bring the effects of self-reflection to bear, we must immediately act on the discoveries made in the process of self-reflection. Unless we convert our thoughts directly into appropriate action and newly foster improved conduct to rectify what is missing or flawed in ourselves, our self-reflection will end in mere thought.

In whatever field or activity, opening up a path means creating new ability. If action does not accompany our thoughts, however, no matter what we think or reflect upon, the new path we have carved out will amount to nothing. We

Dr. Suzuki with his wife, Waltraud, at the Talent Education Institute.

must, therefore, create in ourselves the ability to take action, to practice—it is imperative that we do not forget this tenet.

Through concerted repetition, we are able to master and turn into ability whatever we wish to learn. I have learned the value of bringing to bear this iron principle in such contexts, too. This is why I emphasize the importance of putting into immediate action even the smallest thoughts we entertain. We must exhort ourselves again and again, and without losing heart, to stick to our goals until they are accomplished. I have discovered on multiple occasions that if we repeat something until it is absorbed and becomes habitual, what we first thought impossible proves itself possible, and formerly closed paths begin to open up.

"If you try it, you will succeed." We must neither take this age-old saying for mere verbiage, nor should we consider it a maxim applicable to others but not ourselves. It is in fact a truth that applies to everyone everywhere.

7

Talent Education
for Violin Playing

A group lesson at summer school.

– 1 –
Memory Training

In Order to Develop Basic Ability

At the Talent Education Preschool (Yōji Gakuen, or literally, "School for Young Children"), in order to achieve optimum human development in our preschool students, we introduce subjects different from those offered by nursery schools and kindergartens in general. That is, we train our students to help them develop skills that will serve as the basis for those abilities that will be necessary to them in future years.

To that end, we offer instruction in brush calligraphy by Mrs. Akiyama Kinjō, art by Instructor Tsukikusa Michiko, and English conversation by Mrs. Junker. We wish our children to flourish unconsciously in the environment provided by each of these teachers, who are outstanding practitioners in their fields of specialization, and by their superior artistic sensibilities and accomplished personalities.

Depending upon their training, preschool children are able to produce surprisingly powerful, beautiful works of calligraphy. Our fine art exhibitions are also drawing attention. We teach our students to write their numbers masterfully, since even though they are nothing more than the 10 cardinal numbers, the children will use them for the rest of their lives.

Early childhood is truly wonderful. The children's English pronunciation is truly identical to that of Instructor Junker. So much so that I often listen to their English with envy!

The most crucial thing I have devised, however, is Talent Education for memory. The ability to memorize—this is one of the most important abilities that human beings must develop.

Training to Learn Things Quickly and Retain Them

I found the following in Master Suzuki Daisetsu's *Zen to wa nani ka* (1959, What Is Zen?):

> Among the characteristics of human existence is the fact that we experience life . . . This is because human beings possess such a thing as memory. Memory is tremendously important, for it is the source of human contemplation and creative thought. As long as human beings have memory, experience is possible, and if experience is possible, there will surely be a path for gradual advancement . . . Memory serves as the basis of experience, and it is because experience exists, one can say, that humans are able to fulfill the reason they are human.

Memory is thus exceedingly important. With training, furthermore, one's increased capacity for memorization will enable one to retain material ever more swiftly and for lengthier periods. To learn instantly and not to forget something once it is learned—this is an ability we are able to nurture in our students.

For example, I believe that children who have good grades at school are those whose memory has developed well above the normal range, and that less successful students are simply those who have not formed this ability. In my view, there is no intrinsic superiority or inferiority in these children. How, then, do we carry out that training at our preschool?

Having Our Students Learn and Recite from Memory Issa's Haiku

Instructor Yano Miwa has been involved for 17 years, since 1949, in our new pedagogy of cultivating ability. She trains our students at the preschool daily to learn and to recite from memory the haiku poems most accessible to children—those of Kobayashi Issa. The children commit to memory, within a year, approximately 170 of Issa's haiku. Glancing back at our 17 years of experience, we see that the children thus trained in memory have all gone off to elementary school and earned stellar grades there.

I would like, here, to present some excerpts from Instructor Yano's report on haiku training:

First Trimester 53 haiku, including the following two:
Snow thaws, it thaws, so calls the pigeon in a tree.
Snow has thawed, and the village streets spill over with children.

Second Trimester 64 haiku, including the following two:
Pop! In the heat a hole snaps open in a rhubarb leaf.
A kitten daintily sets its paw, holding a leaf in place.

Third Trimester 45 haiku, including the following two:
Crawl and smile away—your second calendar year starts this morning.
In a home village spring snowflakes mingle with rice, pounded into new year's cakes.

Even children who at first could not learn a haiku after 10 repetitions are able, once into the second trimester, to recite one after three or four repetitions. By the third trimester, some children are able to commit a haiku to memory upon hearing it just once.

We chose the haiku according to the seasons so that they would be easily incorporated into other activities, such as observing nature, singing, and dancing. At the end of each trimester, the entire class recites in unison all of the haiku they learned during that trimester.

Beginning to Compose Issa-Style Haiku

Practicing day after day in this manner, in due course the children begin to converse, or express what they have seen and heard, in a haiku mode; for example, by constantly inserting vocative and emotive particles like *ya* and *kana* in their speech, or by uttering such expressions as *harusame ya* ("ah, this spring rain") and *samidare ya* ("oh, this early summer rain").

The parents and we teachers have made note of and written down a number of the children's poems. Following are some of the Issa-style haiku by the students:

> I wake in the morning and find on the hand-washing basin: a snail.
>
> On the glass window by the bathtub, look, a single snail.
>
> A bicycle pedals away, a branch of cherry blossoms held alongside.
>
> Waking in the morning, a puff of smoke first—my grandpa.
>
> In the twilight sky, twinkle, twinkle, a star appears.
>
> Bigger than a dahlia after all, my face is.
>
> A wind chime in the summer breeze, as my father naps.
>
> Down, down, rain—I can't play outdoors.
>
> The narcissuses stretch taller and taller, and spring is here!
>
> An infant sparrow, gazing at a pretty flower.

Children who develop in this manner apparently do not forget this skill. I have heard their homeroom teachers comment about our students that even after they have advanced to elementary school, they like to add haiku to their illustrated diaries and such.

Above, then, I have discussed some of our activities outside the arena of violin instruction, aimed at molding the human capacities of young children. Let me now turn to the question of how we foster ability in our violin students.

– 2 –
Putting Fun-Seeking Minds to Good Use

Instruct the Parents before Teaching Their Children

When we admit a young child to our studios, we do not let the child play the violin right away. Rather, we begin lessons by first coaching the parent to learn a piece in order to ensure that she will serve as a good home teacher for the child. We also have the child listen to a recording of the piece at home before actually taking up the instrument.

A child develops through home practice. Thus, in order to help the child learn to play with good posture and to practice effectively, it is necessary for the parent to experience the process first. This helps the child to develop properly and successfully.

Our policy is not to allow the child to play the violin until the parent can play an entire piece through. This policy of ours carries tremendous significance. For even if a parent wants to have his child learn the violin, no child at age three or four is consumed with the thought, "I want to practice the violin!"

Thus, what is necessary is to lead the child to wish spontaneously, "I want to try that too!" So, at home, have the child listen to a recording of beginner pieces every day, and at the lesson, place the child among other children who are playing the violin—the point is to create that kind of environment for the child. Moreover, the child's mother is playing a tiny violin better suited to the child, both at the lesson and at home. As a natural result, the child begins to wish to take the instrument from his mother so that he, too, can "have fun:"

"I already know the melody. Other children around me are already playing. I want to play (have fun), too."

Such a desire gradually germinates in him.

Encouraging the Child's Desire to Have Fun with the Violin

Having created the situation just described, we start formal lessons in the following manner.

"Would you like to begin the violin, too?" the parent asks.

"Yes," the child will answer.

"Will you practice well?"

"Yes."

"Then, I will ask the teacher to teach you, too."

Given this, the result is bound to be successful. When the child has learned to play somewhat, you let her play together with other children. What joy this initial experience offers in a young life!

"I can play, too. Now, I can *have fun* with everyone! . . . "

A parent who understands this mode of perception in children will be a superb instructor. The lessons we offer include both individual lessons and group lessons. Parents who do not understand the feelings of children consider their payment of monthly tuition fees as going toward the individual lessons, and they regard the group lessons as nothing more than playtime for the children. Therefore, although they are serious about individual lessons, they allow their child to skip group lessons.

However, the greatest joy for children is playing together with other children. To play alongside more advanced students—how much influence they receive and how well they develop through this experience! This is the true form of education.

Begin with Fun, Then Guide Children Through the Pleasure of Having Fun

"My child refuses to practice at home." Quite a few mothers bring this complaint to me. That is because they fail to understand that their children's motivation in learning the violin stems from the sense that the violin is *fun*, and that they, too, want *to have fun*. "I'm paying tuition every month, to have the training turned into *playing*? That's just . . . "—that is how the adults feel. In other words, calculation enters into education, and that calculation dominates the process. The failure rate is very high in those cases.

Start the child off with the pleasure of having fun, and steer her in the right direction by taking advantage of the pleasure of having fun—no matter what the area, this is where early education must start.

Little Kasuya Hitomi—this is a child who grew up playing the violin every day for three hours a day, starting at the tender age of three. A three-year old?! How is that even possible? This may be what many of you are asking yourselves.

Hitomi's mother gave her a violin instead of a doll, and had her listen over and over to the pieces she was learning, in effect as so-called background music. Hitomi entertained herself all day long with the violin, playing away on it as if it were a toy. Her mother gave her a bit of proper guidance now and then, in accordance with our instructions. The mother, too, joined in on her daughter's fun. This is an embodiment of the masterful art of education.

Our aim needs to be the nurturing of children. The moment we rigidly convince ourselves, "Education is what we're after," we warp a child's development.[1] First foster the heart, then help the child acquire ability. This is indeed nature's proper way.

Young Kasuya Hitomi, thus having been nurtured vibrantly, accompanied us to the United States in 1964, when she was five, carrying her tiny violin in her arms.

Five Minutes per Day and Three Hours per Day

In contrast to the cases of children who resist home lessons, we can point to many examples in which, as a result of a mother's intelligent guidance, daily violin practice occurs at home as a matter of course.

At the summer school one year, I noticed a child of about six years of age who was confidently, and with excellent tone, playing a Vivaldi concerto. "How long has she been playing?" I asked the mother. "A year and a half," she responded.

"She's developing quite nicely. How much does she practice every day?"

---

[1] The Sino-Japanese word for education (kyōiku) is composed of the two characters kyō (教, to teach) and iku (育, to raise, develop, foster).

"About three hours."

Naturally so, I thought. It's easy to tell when a child practices well—she moves differently, and her tone sounds different. More hours of training accumulated in service of a proper method. This is the principle of ability development, with fidelity to the principle inevitably resulting in the cultivation of proper, superior ability.

When you compare someone who practices five minutes a day with someone else who practices three hours a day, even though both learners may be practicing daily without fail, the difference between them is enormous. Ability simply does not develop in the face of insufficient hours of practice. At the same time, whatever hours of effort a learner expends will truthfully be reflected in his development.

Indeed, it would take nine long years for the learner who practices five minutes daily to try to match the results achieved in a mere three months by his fellow learner who practices three hours daily. This is what the math tells us when we calculate out everything. When one learner accomplishes in three months what it takes the other nine years to do, there is no reason for noteworthy ability to develop in the latter.

Young Kasuya Hitomi, as I mentioned, practiced three hours a day, but she was not our only student to do so; Etō Toshiya, Toyoda Kōji, Kobayashi Kenji, and Shida Tomiko also practiced three hours daily, if not more.

Ability Development Is Absolutely Truthful

"I've been practicing for five years," someone may claim, but it is hard to infer anything from this information alone. The question is the quality of daily practice undertaken during that period.

"I've studied for five whole years and I'm still at this level," he says, but if he practices no more than five minutes a day, that daily effort amounts to a mere 150 hours. This person should instead say, "I've put in 150 hours in five years, but somehow I'm not improving." If that's the case, then his problem instantly becomes clear. Under such circumstances, it is only natural that he is languishing. Worse, if he shuts his eyes to the obvious and assumes that the matter comes down to innate ability, then improvement is out of the question.

Ability development is unfalsifiable; it is something that we may view with absolute faith. Thorough training that utilizes a proper and worthwhile approach fosters admirably superior ability. Conversely, training that employs an improper approach develops ability so clumsy that others cannot even begin to imitate it.

To walk a proper, superior path.

To train ever greater hours.

The cultivation of superior ability will invariably result in any person who undertakes the combination of these two endeavors. I am able to declare this without any hesitation whatsoever, based on my personal observation of the development of several thousand children over the past 20 years, coupled with the superiority or inferiority of their parents and teachers.

– 3 –
Calling Out to Children's Vital Forces

Aspiring to Ever Higher Quality

The first piece our young students learn is the "Twinkle Variations." Only after hearing a recording of the piece at home every day does a child learn to play it on the violin. Carefully, carefully, she practices. Once the child has learned to play the entire piece, the teacher will say, "Aha, now you're able to play 'Twinkle' all the way through! Let's move on, then. We're going to start you on lessons for *playing 'Twinkle' extremely well.*"

This is indeed a most crucial point, aimed at heightening the quality of the child's ability. It marks the beginning of lessons in pursuit of better tone, more precisely executed motor functions, and increasingly refined musicality. Using these teaching materials, we foster ability. This approach of ours enables all of our students, without exception, to acquire solid proficiency. Their tone gradually improves, their movements grow ever more fluid and dynamic, and their performances become more and more musical. Ability, in other words, develops.

I am convinced that every child grows to become respectable, and I have never once been betrayed by this conviction. I am determined to help every child become praiseworthy. Unless I do this, I cannot live with myself. In order to confirm whether our students are developing their abilities, I conduct tests of various kinds. Below for example is one game I play with them to assess their proficiency.

How Many Legs Do You Have?

To children who are already able to play the "Twinkle Variations" with sufficient ease I give the following instructions while they play the piece: "All right, let's have a game. You're going to answer my questions while playing the violin, ok? Be sure to answer loudly, and don't stop playing, whatever happens."

I then raise my voice to ask them, "How many legs do you have?"

Amused, the children answer in unison at the top of their lungs, "Two!"

Of course, if they can do this while correctly playing the piece, it means that the ability they have acquired is soundly developed. If there is a child among them whose ability has not yet been sufficiently fostered, it will take everything in him simply to continue playing, with the result that he is unable to utter a syllable. If he nevertheless produces an answer, his hands stop playing.

"How many eyes do you have?"

"Two!"

"How many noses?"

"One!"

Even as the children continue to play through "Twinkle," laughing sweetly away, they are further developing the capacity to enjoy such games with me. Everyone, without fail, develops in this manner. And this acquired ability nudges their overall ability to an even higher plane. This is no different than the fact that we all have the ability to handle a variety of tasks while speaking Japanese without mishap.

There is another testing game that the children enjoy playing. I frequently try this Talent Education approach, in part to discover how much ability our students have acquired and to gauge the level to which their intuitive powers have been heightened. This is a game in which I involve 10 to 15 children, or, depending on the location, 40 to 50 children, having them play together as a group. Let me introduce two or three variants on the game.

Wind Up the Springs in Your Brain!

I clap once or twice the rhythm of no more than the opening two or three bars of a piece. I choose from among the 20 or 30 pieces the children already know how to play, and clapping out its melody, I tell them, "Get ready!" They prepare themselves to start playing together. "Now!" I call out, and the children's bows move simultaneously. They produce exactly the piece I clapped. On rare occasions, they cannot guess the piece and nobody plays a single note.

"Wind up your motor springs!" I then urge them. The children use their right hands to pretend to wind up the springs in their brains, and, wanting to guess successfully this time, they wait for me to clap out the next piece.

With another such game, I stand empty-handed before the children and adopt a violin-playing posture, then mime just once the opening section of a piece. The children closely watch the movement of my hands. When I call out, "Get ready . . . now!" the correct piece resounds from their violins.

"Raise your hands if you couldn't start playing," I tell them. A few hands come up.

"Wind up your motors!" I command the children. Giggling, they wind the springs in their brains, using their right hands. It is truly as if they are playing a happy game. In the midst of all this, their intuitive powers are gradually being trained.

Calling Out to Children's Vital Forces

With more advanced students, the test-game methods become more sophisticated. Here is a game intended to assess, and also cultivate, higher intuitive powers.

"Attention, now! You're going to play with me, ok? It's this piece!"

I say "this piece" without mentioning it by name. The children can only discern what it might be from the posture I take as I bring up my violin, and from the spirit I show. The 10 or so children arrive, as one, at exactly the same posture as me, and exhibit the same spirit.

When I call out, "Here we go!" and start to play, the children instantly join in with me from the opening note. They hardly ever play the wrong piece. Every child develops in this way. On occasion, however, someone may start playing a different piece from the rest of us. That is because the child's brain has taken over. It's the result of her mind thinking, "Oh, I'm sure it's such-and-such piece!"

They succeed if they mindlessly join in with the sound I produce.[2] If they set their minds free, they know the piece by intuition the moment they catch my first note. This is how our beings, our life forces, communicate with each other. We want to foster our children so that they are capable of this kind of empathy; this is what I call "education toward life."

If we continue to nurture in children this kind of practical ability—that is to say, acquired ability over which they have free command—then, assisted by this ability, such children will eventually develop to a level that allows them to demonstrate outstanding ability in any field.

---

[2] The Japanese word rendered here as "mindlessly" is *mushin* (無心), a Zen term that literally means "no-heart" or "no-mind," and refers to a state of freedom from preconceived notions, and from psychological or physical attachments.

8 Having Come This Way, and Now

An embrace with Maestro Casals.

– 1 –
A Magnificent Home Concert

A Fact That Astonishes the World

Over 20 years have passed since the Talent Education movement began training young children on the violin. Here in Japan, now, young children with small violins start, from the age of three or four, to develop an elevated sensibility and a beautiful heart through exposure to the music of Bach and Mozart. By now the number of children so fostered is in excess of 200,000. No such country exists anywhere else in the world.

Shortly before his death in 1955, the Catholic priest Father Sauveur Candau was moved by a grand ensemble of a thousand children playing in unison at the Tokyo Metropolitan Gymnasium, and declared, "A miracle has come to pass!" People worldwide are now expressing great surprise and interest in what is occurring in Japan. From among my own numerous unforgettable memories, I would like to recount a few.

From Momentary Surprise to Powerful Emotion

This particular event took place one evening in 1959. I was awaiting with 30 children the arrival of the world-renowned Vienna Academy Chorus.[1] The location was the Matsumoto Academy of Music, the headquarters of the Talent Education movement, which had been initiated 14 years earlier, in late 1945. We were renting a two-story building from the Matsumoto Traditional Arts Center.

Before long, the bus arrived that was to have transported the choir members after their matinee concert in Matsumoto. The singers did not disembark from the bus for quite some time, however. What they saw was an ordinary city house, except for a sign at the entrance that read, "Matsumoto Academy of Music," in Japanese. There was nothing to suggest to them that this was the music school at which they had an appointment. They were at a loss, wondering if they had been brought to the wrong place.

I went over to the bus to explain, and ushered the members of the choir into our 80-mat banquet room on the second floor. Soon the small violins of 30 preschool and elementary school students began playing Bach's *Double Concerto*. For a second, great surprise registered on the chorus members' faces. They were taken aback by the unexpectedly artistic performance of a challenging work by Bach pouring forth with such beautiful tone from the violins of children so young. Their initial amazement, however, instantly turned into a swell of emotion. After the children had played another two or three pieces, Professor Thomas Christian David (1925–2006), the conductor, turned to tell me, "Amazing . . . this is simply unthinkable. I'd like now to hear the younger ones in the front row play alone. May I call upon some?"

When I replied, "Please go ahead," he asked Hayano Ryūgo in the first row, "Would you give us a solo?"

---

[1] The Wiener Singakademie was founded in 1858. Among its many notable directors was the young Brahms, who moved to Vienna in 1862 to be its choirmaster.

A Sumptuous, Dream-Like Home Concert

Ryūgo was a first grader. "I'll play a Bach concerto," he stated, and performed the *Violin Concerto No. 1 in A Minor*. It was a fine performance. The members of the chorus exchanged looks of surprise.

Next was the youngest child, Narai Kazuko. "Let's hear you play a piece, too," Professor David requested of her. Kazuko announced cheerfully, "I'll play the Vivaldi *Concerto in G Minor*," and played it well. Thoroughly delighted and touched, the chorus members lined up by the piano after consulting with the conductor, saying, "Now we'd like to sing for you."

We had not even dreamed of such a thing. A beautiful chorus singing wonderfully in mixed voices . . . The humble hall of the Matsumoto Academy of Music was instantly turned into the setting of a lavish home concert. This intimate concert by the world's Vienna Academy Chorus and rural Japanese children—it was a joyously unforgettable evening.

A Perfect Manifestation of Youth

Georges Duhamel (1884–1966) is a representative contemporary Frenchman, active in the fields of poetry, drama, fiction, and cultural criticism. On a visit to Japan in 1953, eight years after Talent Education was founded, he heard a violin performance by students of Instructor Nishizaki Shinji, of the Nagoya chapter, and published the following words, referring to the children as "indeed a perfect manifestation of youth":

If I were in a position to offer advice to visitors to Japan or those who attempt to critique Japan, I would wish to tell them to go first to Nagoya. The reason is that I discovered something astonishing here in this city.

I had occasion to listen to the violin performance of a dozen children after lunch in the dining room of Asahi Hall in Nagoya. When the boys and girls, ranging in age from about six to ten, appeared with their little violins, I first assumed that this must be some kind of childlike amusement.

But, conducted by a young teacher, they played a Vivaldi concerto. And what a fine performance it was! I was more dumbfounded than simply moved, for this was indeed a perfect manifestation of youth. Frankly speaking, it was the first time in my life that I witnessed young children demonstrating such musical accomplishment.

The children then played some Bach, their facial expressions conveying innocence. The demanding polyphonic work required precision and refinement, but here, too, they were admirably successful. Last, a young girl, the best player among the group, performed Mozart dynamically and with artistic passion. The work was one that even acknowledged masters find tricky, but she played it accurately and beautifully. And that is not all. In this single city of Nagoya, I learned, there are no less than several hundred such little violin-wielding artists who are unfazed by the challenges of polyphony.

As a traveler from the West, I was amazed by the precocious demonstration of ability in these young children, but at the same time it reminded me of the undercurrent of a traditional sensibility that has been nurtured within the Japanese people.

Although these children face the disadvantage of living in Japan, an Asian nation, they are being trained to a level reached only by the most outstanding Western children. In my view, Japan is indeed the Far West. I dare say, even, that the Japanese are the most Western of Oriental peoples.

– 2 –
Casals Wept

"Oh . . . Oh . . . " the Tears Welled Up

It was 10 o'clock on the morning of April 16, 1961, eight years after Duhamel's visit. Four hundred children, around ages five to twelve, were neatly lined up, their small violins in hand, on the stage of the Bunkyō Public Hall in Tokyo.

The children were awaiting the arrival of the cellist Pablo Casals, one of the greatest artists of the twentieth century. His car pulled up at the front entrance at two minutes before 10, and exactly at 10, Maestro and Marta Casals entered the hall, welcomed by the heartfelt applause of the children's parents and Talent Education instructors. The moment he entered, Casals, catching sight of the 400 children on stage, exclaimed, "Oh . . . oh . . . "; the couple waved their hands high above their heads as they settled into their seats. At the same moment, the "Twinkle Variations" began to resound from the stage.

A lively violin performance by the 400 young children ensued. The old maestro's eyes revealed surprise, and he uttered one deeply felt "Oh . . ." after another. The emotive response of the couple reached its peak shortly afterward, when the children performed a Vivaldi concerto and Bach's *Concerto for Two Violins*. Casals was weeping, I noticed—his eyes were teary and his mouth contorted with emotion . . .

A little later, 15 or 16 students of Instructor Satō Yoshio, who had studied the cello with Casals, performed a handful of pieces such as Saint-Saëns' "The Swan" and Bach's "Bourrée." What must have been the thoughts of the great maestro, as he gazed at these disciples of his disciple!

The Most Touching Scene

When the children's performances were over, I stood by Maestro Casals and started to say, "Thank you very kindly for listening," but before I could finish my sentence, he threw his arms about my shoulders. He remained speechless, tears coursing down his cheeks onto my shoulder.

I cannot say how many times I myself had cried at witnessing similar exuberance in the lofty, unselfconscious expression of life in children. Now the great 75-year-old maestro was shedding tears in response to the tonal expression of their exalted life forces . . . it was a moment of ineffable solemnity.

Maestro Casals then walked with Mrs. Casals toward the children onstage. Patting the youngsters on their heads, he stepped to center stage. Chairs had been placed there for the couple, and they were presented with bouquets by the children. The Casals took their seats, surrounded by endearing Japanese children, and the maestro turned toward the microphone. He raised his voice, quivering with emotion, to address everyone gathered in the hall. "Ladies and gentlemen," he started, "I am now witnessing the most touching kind of scene possible for human beings to encounter." He then continued his remarks along the following lines as I recall them.

The Heart of Hearts That Human Civilization Now Needs

What we have experienced here in these moments seems to me to bear a far greater significance than what is immediately apparent on the outside. Nowhere else in the world am I able to observe at this tremendous a level the spirit of love and sincerity demonstrated here. During my visit to this country, I have felt in every moment the manifestation of a heartfelt demand for a better world. In particular, I have been most impressed by the pursuit of life's most precious values.

How wonderful it is that adults are offering children as young as these the opportunity to take their first steps in life with a lofty mind and noble conduct. Moreover, the method for this is *music*. The children are being trained through music, and forming an understanding of music . . .

Music exists neither to enable dancing nor for seeking out small pleasures, but instead is the most exalted thing in life. Perhaps it is music that will save the world.

Instead of merely saying "congratulations" to the teachers and parents here, I would like at this time to extend my heartiest admiration, profoundest respect, and greatest blessings. I am also grateful for the happiness of adding one additional comment: Japan is not only marvelous in terms of conduct, industry, and art, but constitutes "a heart of hearts." And this heart is what human civilization right now needs first . . . first and foremost, above all else.

– 3 –
In the United States

The Talent Education Movement Expands

Talent Education has seen 20 years come and go. Without my even being aware of it, this movement has now stirred up a sensation in America, where it is discussed more widely and extensively than in Japan. The driving force behind this development turns out to have been a man named Mochizuki Kenji, now on the staff of the Japanese Consulate General in New York City.

Over a span of 10 years, Mr. Mochizuki, unbeknownst to me, became acquainted with our Talent Education movement as a student at Oberlin College, and striving to plant a seedling of this movement there, he "remained in the States," according to a letter he sent me, "solely for that purpose." He managed after considerable effort to obtain a copy of a seven-minute film, taken at one of our mass concerts in Tokyo, of a children's performance of Bach's *Double Violin Concerto*, and introduced it to American specialists. His screening of the film served as the spark for the subsequent inauguration of the Talent Education movement in America.

The first proactive responses to the film came from Professor John Kendall of the music department at Southern Illinois University and Professor Clifford Cook of Oberlin College.[2] Six years ago, Professor Kendall traveled throughout Japan to observe various local chapters, and he also stayed in Matsumoto for a month. Following his return to the United States, he published the English language edition of my *Suzuki Violin School* lesson books and lectured all over the U.S., thereby spreading the Talent Education movement throughout America.

Four years ago, Professor Cook also made a tour of Japan and spent some time in Matsumoto for concerted study. At present, many young students are developing successfully in an experimental classroom that employs the Talent Education method at Oberlin College.

Mochizuki Kenji, the instigator behind all of this, wrote to me, I believe in 1961, to the effect that, "Hereafter, I will do my utmost to ensure that you are able to visit the United States."

Concerts and Lectures in 16 Cities

In the U.S., it was believed that a child cannot, and will not, study the violin before the age of eight or nine. Nevertheless, people were witnessing a performance of Bach's intricate *Concerto for Two Violins* by 800 Japanese children—including five-year-olds who had begun the violin at age two or three. It is not hard, then, to imagine how great the amazement was.

---

[2] John Kendall was teaching at Muskingum College (Ohio, now Muskingum University) when he made his first trip to Japan in 1959. He joined the faculty at Southern Illinois University, Edwardsville, in 1963.

In 1965, portions of our Grand National Concert were broadcast on European television. In a letter from Berlin, Toyoda Kōji told me, in reference to the response of viewers beholding the sight of 1,800 children in Tokyo playing en masse: "People were astonished by that grand performance, and exclaim that they can hardly believe it."

Mr. Mochizuki's promise came to fruition three years later, thanks to an invitation from the American String Teachers Association. Nineteen of us, including 10 children ranging in age from five to thirteen, embarked in 1964 on a concert and lecture tour throughout the U.S. During the three-week tour, we were always on the move, our itinerary calling for us to fly to every corner of the country; we visited 16 universities and presented 26 lectures and concerts.

The children were from the prefectures of Nagano, Niigata, and Aichi, and from greater metropolitan Tokyo. We had simply gathered together anyone who was able to make the arrangements to join the tour. That being the case, I thought I would have them rehearse together once we arrived at our destination. Despite my best intentions, however, the children, who had just barely met each other for the first time, had to line up onstage for their initial performance without the benefit of ever having practiced together.

The performances were televised every night. Everywhere we went, there was a tremendous excitement.

Suzuki Method Grand Concert at Budōkan Hall in Tokyo.

More Than a Revolution in Violin Teaching

Our schedule was so tight that the children's first appearance onstage at the University of Washington wound up being a combination performance and group class, but with each concert the children's performances improved.

A while into each concert, members of the audience would be dabbing at their eyes with their handkerchiefs. Returning from their seats in the audience to the waiting room after the performances, even the mothers accompanying us as chaperones (there were four of them) would be in tears. "With all those Americans crying," they explained, "we couldn't help but get weepy too."

Newsweek magazine, in the article "Fiddling Legions" from its March 23, 1964 issue, reported on the children's performances across the United States in the following manner:

Seven-year-old Asako Hata playfully dropped a chunk of ice down her neighbor's back, and the long table of children at lunch one day last week burst into delighted giggles. Forty minutes later, Asako was standing on the stage of New York's august Juilliard School of Music, bobbing her head shyly to acknowledge the thunderous clapping that greeted her performance of a complicated Veracini violin sonata.

The solo climaxed a concert that was at once impressive and absurd, in which 10 tiny Japanese children, ranging in age from 5 to [13] played Bach and Vivaldi that drew bravos from a highly critical audience of Juilliard students and faculty. If their applause was tinged with sentimentality (when the children's teacher, Professor Shinichi Suzuki, stepped on stage to tune a 5-year-old's [eighth]-size violin, the audience sighed), it was nonetheless wholly deserved. "This is amazing," said Juilliard violin Professor Ivan Galamian. "They show remarkable training, a wonderful feeling for the rhythm and flow of music."

. . . Although about five percent of Suzuki's students make careers in music, the 65-year-old professor insists: "I just want to make good citizens. If a child hears good music from the day of his birth, and learns to play it himself, he develops sensitivity, discipline and endurance. He gets a beautiful heart . . . If nations cooperate in raising good children, perhaps there won't be any war."

Suzuki has done more than revolutionize violin teaching in Japan. Oberlin Professor Clifford Cook says:

"What Suzuki has done for young children earns him a place among the benefactors of mankind, along with Schweitzer, Casals, and Tom Dooley."[3]

---

[3] Thomas Anthony Dooley III (1927–1961) was a U.S. Navy physician in the 1950s widely known for his work in evacuating refugees fleeing from North to South Vietnam, and for setting up medical clinics and hospitals in Vietnam and Laos during and after his military service. He died of cancer at the age of 34.

Epilogue: My Dream

So That Everyone May Attain Happiness

I entertain for all people a sense of friendship and respect. Particularly when it comes to interacting with young children, I cannot help but do so with friendliness and respect. Additionally, I have come to live my days with the heartfelt prayer, "May every child born on this earth become an upstanding human being, a happy individual, and a person with desirable abilities." This is because I came to realize that every child, without exception, is born with the potential to do so.

People ask me, "What's the use of racing about with such an impossible dream?" I believe, however, that it *is* possible, that the time will surely come when humankind creates such a world, and that one day people everywhere will recognize the potential of children. This is why, after Maestro Casals spoke on world peace at the United Nations, I did not hesitate to expound on this dream before the delegates in attendance from the many nations of the world.

In the real world, too, in every arena where I could lend my strength, I have committed my entire being to the pursuit of Talent Education: I have had a sympathetic elementary school principal set up an experimental classroom in which the aim was to design a pedagogical method that produced no dropouts, I have sought the opportunity to care for brain-damaged children, and I also make a point of discussing national policies for child care when mingling with thoughtful legislators and financiers who possess the wealth and position to realize my ideas.

An Important Dream That Is No Mere Dream

The Children's Charter declares that every child shall receive protection.[1] And if the world abides by this proclamation, then my dream will be no mere dream. Moreover, this is the most important task that we humans on earth can achieve.

I would like to see a true national policy for child-rearing that protects and nurtures every single infant—indeed, this was my primary and deeply felt motivation in starting the Talent Education movement. Each and every child has the capacity to develop well; it all rests on how the child is fostered.

As a result of poverty, sometimes babies who should develop well are failed by the adults around them. Unwholesome environments can also lead to failed attempts to nurture babies. In order to prevent such occurrences, I would like to see assistance made available under the auspices of the state.

For that to happen, I believe that, as with police officers who are assigned to particular areas that they patrol, the state should train and deploy child-care counselors throughout the country to be responsible for dispensing child-rearing guidance in every Japanese home. I would like, in this way, for the nation to expend its utmost effort so that all children prior to starting compulsory education may develop robustly.

I am hopeful that by reading this book you have come to understand how wonderfully young children can develop, depending on how they are fostered. To my mind, it is irresponsible to accept the validity of the proverb, "A three-year-old's soul remains the same even at age one hundred," simply by looking at the results of developments that have already taken place in someone. Age three, that is to say, early childhood, is a decisive period for human formation. I believe, therefore, that the task of protecting and fostering young children, without mishap, is something that must absolutely be undertaken, by a nation's 100-year plan, or, for that matter, for the sake of the future of humankind.[2]

---

[1] This Children's Charter (Jidō Kenshō in Japanese) is a reference to the World Child Welfare Charter (Sekai Jidō Fukushi Kenshō in Japanese), endorsed by the League of Nations in 1924 and by the United Nations in 1946. The Charter's principles were first espoused in 1923, in a proclamation drafted by social reformer Eglantyne Jebb (1876–1928) and known as the Geneva Declaration of the Rights of the Child.

[2] The reference to a 100-year plan reflects the common saying, originating from the writings of the 7th-century BCE Chinese philosopher Guan Zhong, that grains take one year of planning for cultivation, trees 10 years, and humans 100 years.

Let's Start Today, Right Now, and Not Hold Off Until Tomorrow

Human civilization up to now is analogous to someone looking at the limp seedlings they have raised and assuming they were genetically weak to begin with, then blithely continuing to cultivate them without attending to the fact that so many of the seedlings are doing poorly. Humankind must some day disengage itself from such folly. The sooner everyone realizes this, the better things will be, and the sooner everyone changes the situation, the closer will true happiness be within the reach of humanity.

I count myself among those humans who were improperly nurtured. Many people have been. From my youth onward, I have continually strived to rehabilitate my flawed self, and thereby overcome my failings. The result is the person I am today.

It is my wish that this book has persuaded you that instead of resigning ourselves to the notion that our shortcomings are innate, we ought to recognize that as long as each of us tries diligently, we are all capable of becoming worthy human beings and of acquiring new abilities.

If you have indeed come to this realization, do not put it off until tomorrow, but today, starting this very moment, please transfer that realization into action. It will bring joy to your daily life. If only everyone could experience this difference—this is yet another happy dream of mine that I must eventually, without fail, make come true.

A bust of Dr. Suzuki.

Research Index

Introduction from the Creator of the Index

Dr. Shinichi Suzuki was one of the most influential pedagogues of the 20th century. The Suzuki® Method is now employed on a global scale, and with increasing popularity. While Suzuki made it clear his goal was not to produce professional musicians, but to develop noble individuals, the method has succeeded on both counts. Many of today's most notable and sought after musicians were trained using the Suzuki® Method. Despite its success, the Suzuki® Method is largely absent from music education research. While music pedagogy theorists like Dalcroze, Kodály, and Orff are the focus of vast amounts of research, Suzuki, for the most part, is ignored. Only of late has there been a slight emergence of research regarding the Suzuki® Method.

Suzuki's wife, Waltraud Suzuki, completed the original translation of *Nurtured by Love* from Japanese to English. In her autobiography, she indicates that *Nurtured by Love* is the text intended to disseminate Dr. Suzuki's teaching philosophy and, as such, is the primary text for research on the Suzuki® Method. However, from a research perspective, *Nurtured by Love* is a challenging text to use. The text is not a systematic description of a pedagogical method, nor is it a chronological account of the method's development. The book is constructed as a series of stories, anecdotes and ideas that led to the development of a philosophy. I strongly believe Suzuki purposefully structured his discourse in this manner so as not to present instructions on how to teach, but rather to inculcate readers with his philosophy. Nevertheless, the organization of this book, whether purposeful or not, makes it difficult to use for research purposes.

While involved in my own research I found myself having to re-read the entire book in order to ensure I was finding everything Suzuki wrote on various topics. Having to re-read *Nurtured by Love Revised Edition* repeatedly certainly has its advantages, but it is also exceedingly time consuming. In order to promote research into the Suzuki® Method, researchers need to have easier access to the information inside *Nurtured by Love*. For that reason, I have created an index for this revised edition to assist anyone interested in researching topics relating to Suzuki pedagogy. The index is presented twice, once by topic, and once alphabetically. The index may seem more substantial than a typical index for a book this size. Because there is so little research dealing with the method, I chose to be liberal when determining what items to include. On numerous occasions Suzuki refers to a person only by their surname. When I was able to establish who these people were, I include their first names as well. If I could not determine who they were with complete confidence, I simply include their appropriate title, i.e.: Mr., Mrs., or Dr.

I believe that this index will assist other researchers in their examination of the Suzuki Method and so I donate it to be used in *Nurtured by Love Revised Edition*. It is my fervent hope that contemporary music education research will continue to focus its interest on the Suzuki® Method, and finally give it the attention it warrants.[1]

Zachary Ebin

---

[1] Readers should not hesitate to contact me if they find an error in the index, or if they feel other items should be added.

Topical Index

Institutions

Texts

Miscellaneous Index

Alphabetical Index

150

151

152